A North American Free Trade Agreement

The Strategic Implications for Canada

Michael Hart

Centre for Trade Policy and Law
Institute for Research on Public Policy

Legal Deposit Third Quarter
Bibliothèque nationale du Québec

Canadian Cataloguing in Publication Data

Hart, Michael M. (Michael Marten), 1944-.
A North American Free Trade Agreement:
The Strategic Implications for Canada

Prefatory material in English and French
Includes bibliographical references

ISBN 0-88645-114-0

1. Canada – Commercial policy. 2. United States – Commercial policy.
3. Mexico – Commercial Policy. 4. Canada – Foreign economic relations.
5. United States – Foreign economic relations. 6. Mexico – Foreign
economic relations. I. Institute for Research on Public Policy. II. Centre
for Trade Policy and Law

The camera-ready copy for this publication was created on an Apple
Macintosh SE-30 using Microsoft Word and printed on an Apple Laserwriter
II. The text is set in the Palatino font. Cover design by Aartvark
Communications of Ottawa. Publication has been facilitated by financial
assistance from the Business Council on National Issues.

Centre for Trade Policy and Law/
Centre de droit et de politique commercial
Room 204, Social Sciences Research Building
Carleton University
Ottawa, Ontario K1S 5B6

The Institute for Research on Public Policy/
L'institut de recherches politiques
P.O. Box 3670 South
Halifax, Nova Scotia B3J 3K6

To

Derek Burney

*whose inspiring leadership gave me the
confidence to pursue my interest in free trade,
with some regret that it could not have been
<u>the</u> book*

Table of Contents

Tables

Charts

Foreword

In the 1980s Canadians from every walk of life were reminded of the importance of trade to the Canadian economy and the critical role of trade agreements in promoting and protecting Canadian interests. For good or for ill, the debate about the Canada-United States Free Trade Agreement brought trade policy out of the closet where it had languished for many years and into the forefront of public policy. Canadians began to take a sudden and urgent interest in issues that only a few years earlier were well understood in only limited circles of the public and private sectors. The resulting debate generated unprecedented and even strident exchanges of views in Canada about fundamental values and perceptions.

Events in Washington and Mexico City over the past few months promise to keep the debate alive. Mexico, having substantially modernized and liberalized its own economy and having observed the outcome of negotiations between Canada and the United States, has now decided that it desires a similar agreement with the United States. This challenge from Mexico raises real and important issues for Canada. Whatever is negotiated between the United States and Mexico will have direct spillover effects on Canada. Canadian trade and investment interests will be affected, whether we like it or not. The issue is whether Canada can afford to stand aside or whether it should join in and help to shape a tripartite North American free-trade agreement.

Over the past decade, the Institute has been in the forefront in Canada in publishing monographs and conference volumes on Canadian interests in the international economy, featuring some of Canada's foremost policy analysts and involving joint ventures with a number of academic centres including the Centre for Trade Policy and Law. This, our second joint publication, provides much needed background and analysis for the issues raised by

vii

Mexican interest in North American free trade. It is a timely, informed and thoughtful contribution to an emerging debate. The significance of this issue for Canada deserves to be much more thoroughly and widely understood, and this as an urgent matter.

Michael Hart is especially well qualified to comment on this issue. A seasoned trade policy practitioner, he was part of the team that negotiated the FTA and for the past three years has been on loan from the federal government to Carleton University where he helped to organize a more intense program of teaching and research on trade policy issues. He has followed events involving Mexico closely and made a number of trips to Mexico and the United States to participate in conferences and seminars on Mexico and its trade relations with the United States and Canada.

While not all students of the subject would agree with the trenchant criticism of the GATT system and its continuing potential, his study provides a provocative and valuable analysis of rapidly evolving events in Mexico, Canada and the United States and should help Canadians decide what direction to take on the issue of North American free trade.

Rod Dobell
President
The Institute for Research
  on Public Policy

J. H. Warren
for the
Centre for Trade Policy
and Law

July, 1990

Avant-Propos

Dans les années 80, on a rappelé aux Canadiens de toutes conditions sociales, l'importance du commerce pour l'économie canadienne et du rôle essentiel des accords commerciaux pour promouvoir et protéger les intérêts canadiens. Pour le meilleur ou pour le pire, le débat concernant l'Accord de libre-échange entre le Canada et les États-Unis a ramené à la surface la politique commerciale, et au premier plan de la politique publique, après qu'elle eut pendant nombre d'années reposé sur les tablettes. Les Canadiens ont commencé à manifester un intérêt soudain et pressant relativement à des questions qui étaient, il y a seulement quelques années, bien connues dans les milieux restreints des secteurs privé et public seulement. Le débat qui s'ensuivit a engendré des échanges d'opinions sans précédent et même virulents au Canada au sujet des perceptions et des valeurs fondamentales véhiculées.

Des événements qui se sont déroulés, à Washington et à Mexico, au cours des derniers mois, promettent de tenir le débat sur la sellette. Le Mexique qui a procédé à une modernisation et une libéralisation importante de sa propre économie et qui a observé les résultats des négociations et des pourparlers qui ont eu lieu entre le Canada et les États-Unis, a maintenant décidé qu'il souhaitait conclure un accord semblable avec les États-Unis. Ce défi, que semble vouloir relever le Mexique, a soulevé plusieurs questions importantes pour le Canada. Quel que soit l'accord négocié entre les États-Unis et le Mexique, celui-ci aura des retombées directes sur le Canada. Le commerce canadien et les intérêts d'investissement seront touchés, que cela nous plaise ou non. La question est de savoir si le Canada peut être mis de côté ou s'il doit faire partie de ces négociations et prêter son aide à l'élaboration d'un Accord de libre-échange nord-américain tripartite.

Au cours de la dernière décennie, l'Institut a été mis au premier plan au Canada en publiant des monographies et des ouvrages sur des conférences traitant des intérêts canadiens sur l'économie internationale, illustrant des politicologues les plus réputés au Canada ainsi qu'un nombre de centres d'études, y compris le Centre de droit et de politique commerciale. Cette deuxième publication conjointe fournit des renseignements pertinents et des analyses extrêmement utiles sur les questions soulevées concernant l'intérêt manifesté par le Mexique envers le libre-échange nord-américain. Celle-ci constitue une contribution sérieuse, pertinente et opportune relative à une question d'actualité. L'importance de cette question pour le Canada mérite d'être mieux comprise et ce, de toute urgence.

Michael Hart est particulièrement bien qualifié pour faire des commentaires sur cette question. Praticien chevronné de politique commerciale, il fit partie de l'équipe qui a négocié l'ALE entre le Canada et les États-Unis et, depuis ces trois dernières années, détaché du gouvernement fédéral, il est à l'emploi de l'Université Carleton où il a participé à l'élaboration d'un programme d'enseignement et de recherche plus approfondi sur les questions afférentes à la politique commerciale. Il a suivi étroitement le déroulement des événements impliquant le Mexique et a fait plusieurs voyages à Mexico et aux États-Unis afin de participer à des conférences et des colloques portant sur le Mexique et ses relations commerciales avec les États-Unis et le Canada.

Bien que tous les intéressés à cette question ne sont pas unanimes quant à la critique mordante dont fait l'objet le système du GATT et du travail qui se poursuit, l'étude de celui-ci donne une analyse valable et stimulante des événements qui évoluent rapidement au Mexique, au Canada et aux États-Unis. Cette analyse devrait aider les Canadiens à décider de la position à prendre sur la question afférente au libre-échange en Amérique du Nord.

Rob Dobell
Le président
Institut de recherches politiques

J. H. Warren
Centre de droit et de
politique commerciale

Juillet 1990

Acknowledgements

My interest in Mexico and the possibility of a North American free-trade agreement started at various conferences where I gave papers explaining the Canada-US FTA and where the Mexicans in the audience always asked if I thought the agreement contained lessons for them. In order to answer these questions, particularly on trips to the US Southwest and then Mexico, I had to find out something about Mexico. What I learned challenged a lot of conventional wisdom.

I learned the extent to which Mexico has unilaterally reformed its economic policies. These reforms have greatly altered the potential for closer economic relations between the three economies of North America. We are witnessing the unfolding of a rare revolution, a bloodless revolution ruthlessly discarding a century of deeply entrenched mercantilism, leaving, as one veteran noted, very few economic cadavers in its wake.

The prospect of either a bilateral US-Mexico free-trade agreement or a trilateral accord involving Canada would rightly have been dismissed as idle speculation just a few years ago. As the revolution has taken hold, however, that prospect has gradually changed. Today, it is no longer a matter of speculation but of urgent policy discussion in all three capitals. A North American accord now appears a distinct possibility.

Having made an investment in learning something about Mexico, I responded eagerly to a request from the Business Council on National Issues to provide some background on the issues that would need to be confronted should Canada decide to join what appeared to be impending US-Mexico free-trade negotiations. With the kind permission of the Council, I have taken that report and expanded it into this study. Along the way, I have benefitted greatly from interviews and discussions with Canadian, US and Mexican officials, businessmen and analysts.

Parts of the study are based on papers I delivered in June, 1989 at a professional seminar sponsored by the Centre for Trade Policy and Law; in October, 1989 at a conference on Region North America at Baylor University in Texas; in November, 1989 at the the annual meeting of CONACEX in Monterey, Mexico; and at the June, 1990 International Forum: Mexico's Trade Options in the Changing International Economy hosted by the Universidad Tecnologica de Mexico in Mexico City. An earlier version of this study was discussed at a meeting organized by the Council on Foreign Relations in New York and I am grateful to Michael Aho of the Council and Murray Smith of the Institute for Research on Public Policy for organizing this meeting. All the participants provided me with sharp and constructive advice. In addition, I would like to thank Bill Dymond, Jock Finlayson, Peter Morici, Konrad von Finckenstein, Jake Warren and Sidney Weintraub for their detailed and helpful comments on various drafts. Whatever faults remain can only be attributed to my obtuseness in not following their advice. Three of my graduate assistants at the Centre for Trade Policy and Law, Keith Martin, Michael Gort and Judith van Walsum, provided invaluable assistance in digging out some of the background and statistical material. Finally, I would like to thank my wife, Mary Virginia, for her unflagging devotion to correct grammar and style in her repeated reviews of the manuscript.

The study examines a rapidly evolving situation. Events in the past few months alone have materially altered assessments of some of the implications of extending the Canada-US FTA to Mexico. Events in the next few months will no doubt require further adjustments in the analysis. Over the next few years, as academic specialists in Canada, the United States and Mexico examine the details and implications of this issue, we will learn much more about what is involved. Until then, however, we will have to be satisfied with less scientific and more "seat-of-the pants" analysis, such as this study. It is to be hoped that it and others to follow, will provide a sufficient basis for the decisions that must be taken and preparations that may be launched over the next few months.

Michael Hart

Ottawa
July 28, 1990

xii

The Author

Michael Hart is Director of the Center for Trade Policy and Law in Ottawa, Canada, on leave from the Canadian foreign service. Educated at Calvin College, the University of Virgina and the University of Toronto, he taught European history at McMaster University and the University of Prince Edward Island before joining the Department of External Affairs in 1974.

After a series of assignments in Ottawa and Geneva, he was asked to manage the Canadian government's 1982-83 trade policy review project and put together the two resulting documents, *A Review of Canadian Trade Policy* and *Trade Policy for the 1980s: A Discussion Paper.*

In 1983 he was seconded to the Institute for Research on Public Policy in Ottawa where he prepared one of the research volumes for the Macdonald Royal Commission, *Canadian Economic Development and the International Trading System,* as well as a short explanation of the bilateral sectoral trade initiative, *Some Thoughts on Canada-U.S. Sectoral Free Trade.*

In 1984, while serving as Director of Domestic Policy in the Air Administration of the Department of Transport, he worked with the staff of the Macdonald Commission in preparing its Final Report. That report, inter alia, recommended that the government negotiate a free-trade agreement with the United States and was instrumental in the government's decision to proceed.

In 1985 he returned to the Department of External Affairs to co-ordinate preparations for the bilateral negotiations and the following year joined the Trade Negotiations Office responsible for contingency protection issues – subsidies, countervailing duties, antidumping duties and safeguards. In the closing stages of the negotiations, he worked with the legal team in drafting the final text and prepared much of the Government's initial explanatory material.

He left the Trade Negotiations Office at the end of 1987 for a period of academic leave, teaching trade policy courses at the University of Western Ontario, Carleton University and the University of Ottawa and in 1989 became founding director of the Centre for Trade Policy and Law, a new centre sponsored jointly by Carleton and Ottawa. While on leave, he has spoken to a wide variety of audiences on trade policy issues and published a number of academic articles.

1

A Challenge from Mexico

On March 17, 1985 US President Ronald Reagan and Canadian Prime Minister Brian Mulroney declared that they were embarking "on a joint effort to establish a climate of greater predictability and confidence for Canadians and American alike to plan, invest, grow and compete more effectively with one another and in the global market."[1] A little less than four years later their two governments implemented into law the Canada-US free-trade agreement, arguably among the most important achievements of the two chief executives.

Less than two years later, on June 11, 1990, Mexican President Carlos Salinas de Gortari and US President George Bush issued an almost identical declaration, committing their two administrations to the negotiation of a comprehensive bilateral trade agreement. In a joint communiqué, the two Presidents indicated that they had instructed their two senior trade officials, Mexican Commerce Secretary Jaime Serra Puche and United States Trade Representative Carla Hills, to start the necessary studies and exploratory discussions preparatory to the possible opening of negotiations sometime early in 1991.[2]

---

[1] "Declaration by the Prime Minister of Canada and the President of the United States of America Regarding Trade in Goods and Services," reproduced in Department of External Affairs, *Canadian Trade Negotiations: Introduction, Selected Documents, Further Reading* (Ottawa: Supply and Services, 1986), p. 13.

[2] See news reports for June 11, 1990 in the *Toronto Globe and Mail* and *The New York Times*.

Mexico, convinced of the value of the Canada-US free-trade agreement, has now issued a challenge to Canada and the United States that it wants to reach a similar accord. The United States has accepted the challenge. Canadian ministers and officials are considering the implications of the challenge for Canada and the possibility of Canadian participation in negotiations leading to a North American free-trade accord. Whatever their ultimate decision, the June 11 announcement in Washington brought home in stark relief the reality of the global marketplace. Decisions and events thousands of miles from home can change Canadian priorities overnight. Until a few months ago, Canadian interest in Mexico did not go far beyond thoughts about winter vacations. Equally, Mexican interest in a free-trade agreement seemed at best a remote possibility only a year ago. We now face the vital necessity of learning everything we can about Mexican trade and economic policy as we enter the next round of free-trade debates.

Table 1
Canada-USA-Mexico
Basic Economic Indicators

	Canada	USA	Mexico
Population (1988; in millions)	26.1	245.9	83.6
Annual growth (1980-88; percent)	0.9	1.0	2.2
Area (000 KM^2)	9,976.0	9,363.0	1,973.0
Total GNP (1988; in billions of US dollars	437.5	4,863.7	151.9
Country Share (percent)	8.0	89.2	2.8
Average annual growth rate in GNP (1980-88)	2.3	2.1	-1.4
GNP per capita (1988; in US dollars)	16,860.0	19,870.0	1,820.0
Structure of production (1985) (distribution of GDP; percent)			
Agriculture	3.0	2.0	11.0
Industry	30.0	31.0	35.0
(Manufacturing)	(16.0)	(20.0)	(24.0)
Services	67.0	67.0	54.0
Export of goods and non-factor services (1988; percent of GNP)	29.0	7.0	16.0
Merchandise trade (billions US dollars)			
Exports (1988)	111.4	315.3	20.8[a]
Imports (1988)	112.2	458.6	19.6[b]

Adapted from Gerardo Bueno, "A Mexican View," in William Diebold Jr., ed., *Bilateralism, Multilateralism and Canada in U.S. Trade Policy* (New York: Council on Foreign Relations, 1988), p. 107. World Bank, *World Tables,* 1989-90 edition.
a.   includes Mexican value-added from Maquiladora industries only.
b.   does not include imports from US re-exported from Maquiladora industries.

Mexican interest in free-trade negotiations with the United States and Canada has grown quickly but surely. In a matter of just a few months, the issue has evolved from a highly speculative and not very burning academic issue in all three countries to a question of pressing policy in government and business circles. The administration of Carlos Salinas de Gortari, elected by a slim majority in 1988, has decided that in order for Mexico to modernize, grow and prosper, it must nurture a market-oriented economy integrated into the world economy. Salinas was the architect of the 1986 decision under President de la Madrid to join GATT and end Mexico's self-imposed economic isolation. As President, he has surrounded himself with an able group of US-educated technocrats who have no fear of closer economic relations with the United States. Salinas himself is a Harvard-educated PhD in political economy and Commerce Secretary Jaime Serra holds a Yale economics doctorate. Both have recruited other US-trained economists and political scientists to their immediate circle of advisors. The success of Salinas' team in bringing inflation down, addressing the debt crisis and attracting new investment suggests that they are on the right track.

Salinas and his technocrats have a long and tough row to hoe. Despite recent reforms, Mexico's economy remains seriously underdeveloped (see Table 1). The gap between rich and poor is enormous and the number of poor is growing rapidly: Mexico's population grew by more than fifteen million in the 1980s. Mexico needs to develop at least a million new jobs a year to keep up with its rapidly growing young labour force. It has to do even better if it wants to reduce unemployment and underemployment. The Mexican economy has long been dominated by a bloated and inefficient public sector and was for years almost wholly dependent on its internal market. The direction Salinas wants to go is widely admired outside of Mexico; within Mexico, political support is neither deep nor widespread. He has made a start but has a long way to go and there remains skepticism that the magic of the market will work for a Mexico that has long depended on government planning and subsidies.[3] To overcome this skepticism and modernize Mexico, he will need outside help.

---

[3]   Salinas' main opponent in the 1988 election, Cuauhtémoc Cárdenas, ran on a platform that emphasized the need to slow down economic reforms and increase dependence on internally led rather than export-led growth. In a recent article "Misunderstanding Mexico," *Foreign Policy*, no. 78 (Spring, 1990), pp. 113-130, he outlines his misgivings about the Salinas program of economic reform and closer trade ties with the United States. A less partisan and more considered view of the issues raised by the Salinas program of "apertura" can be found in Jorge G. Castañeda, "The Choices Facing Mexico," in Susan Kaufman Purcell, *Mexico in Transition: Implications for U.S. Policy* (New York: Council on Foreign Relations, 1988), pp. 18-27.

Salinas can count on strong support from the Mexican business sector.[4] It knows that the way of the past is no longer viable and that Mexico must look beyond its borders for solutions. Mexican manufacturers, convinced that they must look beyond Mexico for their future, have found some things they liked but also some concerns. They welcome the opportunities presented by the US, Japanese and European markets but have found that access to them is neither as open nor as secure as they might like. They look at GATT negotiations as holding much promise for the future but less prospect for a short-term payoff. They have concluded that in order to invest in a future based on foreign trade and investment, they need more open and secure access to their principal market, that of the United States, and they need it immediately. Their attitude should have a familiar ring for Canadians.

For both the Mexican government and Mexican industrialists, a more open trading regime is clearly a means to an end. The end is a more prosperous Mexico nurtured by Mexican and foreign investment. That investment will only come if private investors are convinced that there will be markets for the products of new investments, with the US market the most promising immediate prospect. Dependence on the internal market or the markets of Latin America has now been dismissed as unrealistic. Similarly, the prospects of more intense trade and investment relations with Europe and across the Pacific are seen as possible in the long-term but not very likely in the 1990s. Indeed, as in the case of Canada, closer trade relations with the United States leading to the development of more competitive industries are regarded as an important precursor to increased trade across the Atlantic and Pacific.

Mexican industrialists and politicians are acutely aware of the political risks of negotiating bilaterally with the United States. They face deeply embedded anti-American sentiments in Mexico, based on a rocky bilateral history with its

---

4   For example, at the November 1989 annual meeting in Monterey of CONACEX (Consejo Nacional de Comercio Exterior), the Mexican equivalent of the Canadian Export Association, talk of the need for a US-Mexico agreement dominated the discussions, including in a speech from Commerce Secretary Jaime Serra. This was not always the case. Before the introduction of the Mexican reform program in 1985, business held a strong stake in Mexico's protectionist regime. The majority now see their future inexorably tied to Mexico's more outward-looking policy mix. Writes Sidney Weintraub: "those favoring protection are fighting a rearguard action rather than being in the vanguard of trade policy, as they were for so many decades." "The North American Free Trade Debate," paper prepared for the International Forum: Mexico's Trade Options in the Changing International Economy, Universidad Tecnologica de Mexico, Mexico City, June 11-15, 1990, p. 3. See also Luis Rubio, "The Changing Role of the Private Sector," in Susan Kaufman Purcell, *Mexico in Transition: Implications for U.S. Policy* (New York: Council on Foreign Relations, 1988), pp. 31-42.

giant neighbour to the north.[5] One way to reduce that risk, however, is to make the negotiations a three-way affair. Canada would provide a politically attractive counterweight to that of the United States in any free-trade arrangement and bring some commercial advantages as well. Additionally, the 1987 Canada-US free-trade agreement provides a convenient point of departure for any negotiations.[6] Both Mexican politicians and business leaders have made these points to their Canadian counterparts.

Mexican expressions of interest in negotiating with the United States would not have meant much if that interest had not been reciprocated by the Bush Administration in Washington. Bush has a strong Texas connection. So do Secretaries Baker and Mosbacher and Senate Finance Chairman Bentsen. All are acutely aware of the strong interest in the US Southwest for a new accommodation with Mexico.[7] A growing proportion of their electorate has strong family and economic ties to Mexico. They are being urged that it is in the US interest to ensure that Mexico remains market-oriented and looks outward rather than inward. They know that 85 million Mexican consumers are not to be dismissed lightly, even if many of them are still poor. They also believe that a free-trade agreement may be the least painful way to address the illegal immigration prob-

---

5   Notes the Bilateral Commission on the Future of United States-Mexico Relations: "The relationship between Mexico and the United States has no counterpart anywhere in the world. Nowhere else do two close neighbours reflect such sharp differences or share such common interests. Imbued with dissimilar cultural legacies, Mexico and the U.S. have traversed divergent historical paths. One is rich, the other not. They have forged contrasting models of social organization. They speak different languages and follow different customs. And they have constructed distinct perspectives on the international arena. This is a remarkable juxtaposition of societies, one that vividly illustrates the gap between the developed and developing worlds." *The Challenge of Interdependence: Mexico and the United States* (New York: University Press of America, 1989), p. 9. See also Sidney Weintraub, *Marriage of Convenience: Relations between Mexico and the United States* (Washington: 1990) and Robert A. Pastor and Jorge G. Castañeda, *Limits to Friendship: The United States and Mexico* (New York: Alfred A. Knopf, 1988).

6   Gerardo Bueno, a leading exponent of a North American Free Trade Agreement, argued as early as 1987 that Canada and the United States should be prepared to contemplate Mexican accession and thus respond to the aspirations of an awakening Mexico. See his "A Mexican View," in William Diebold Jr., ed., *Bilateralism, Multilateralism and Canada in U.S. Trade Policy* (New York: Council on Foreign Relations, 1988), pp. 105-127.

7   This view has been developed in considerable detail by Sidney Weintraub, now Dean Rusk Professor at the Lyndon Baines Johnson School of Public Affairs at the University of Texas in a series of books and articles starting with *Free Trade Between Mexico and the United States* (Washington: Brookings Institution, 1984) through *A Marriage of Convenience: Relations Between Mexico and the United States* (New York: Oxford University Press, 1990). A former State Department official stationed in Mexico, Weintraub has developed a deep love and understanding of Mexico tempered by a realistic assessment of what is feasible and negotiable in relations between the two countries.

lem and the trade in illicit drugs. They think it will be better to provide long-term opportunities for Mexicans in Mexico through increased trade and investment than to try to stop the daily hemorrhage at the border, and they believe Mexican officials are more likely to cooperate with US officials in cracking down on the drug trade within the framework of hope offered by a free-trade agreement.

Table 2
The Structure of North American Merchandise Trade

	Canada	USA	Mexico
Structure of exports (percent)	*1987*	*1987*	*1985*
Agriculture	7.1	8.6	9.7
Mining and Quarrying	11.8	2.6	57.2
Manufacturing	81.1	88.8	35.7
Food	3.4	5.2	1.5
Textiles	1.0	2.1	1.7
Wood & Products	5.8	0.9	0.3
Paper & Products	11.7	3.1	0.6
Chemicals	8.0	14.1	8.8
Non-Metal Minerals	0.6	0.7	1.4
Basic Metal	6.2	1.6	2.7
Metal Manufacturing	42.5	53.1	17.8
Other Manufactures	1.7	8.0	0.8
Structure of imports (percent)			
Food	5.6	7.1	9.7
Industrial Supplies	20.4	19.0	36.5
Fuels	4.8	11.0	3.8
Machinery	22.2	18.9	32.6
Transport equipment	33.8	22.1	10.9
Consumer Goods	11.1	20.2	6.3
Miscellaneous	2.1	2.6	0.1

Source: United Nations, *International Trade Statistics Yearbook*, Volume 1, *Trade by Country*, 1987.

Washington opinion makers are not minimizing the difficulty of negotiating a free-trade agreement between two countries at very different stages of economic development. Nor are they ignorant of the legacy of a troubled Mexican-American past. Here again they believe that Canada can be helpful. Senior American policy makers have suggested that the United States would welcome a trilateral negotiation. But the United States has also indicated it cannot move until it hears from Mexico and Canada. The initiative cannot come from Washington. Launching negotiations will require some delicate maneuvering given the complexity and inwardness of US trade law combined with the sensitivities in Mexico and Canada of too much public US interest. Mexico has now made its interest plain; the US Administration has made its initial commitment; the next move is up to Canada.

For Canadians the strategic question, therefore, is how should Canada respond? Should Canada stand back and await further developments or should it take a more active position and seek a seat at the table from the outset? Should Canada play an active role in the initial exploratory discussions or only act once the US-Mexico situation becomes clearer? Are Canadian goals purely defensive or are there interests in the United States and Mexico that can be advanced by participating in the negotiations?

The Canadian interest can only be examined in light of the strong interest in Mexico and the US in a bilateral agreement and the existence of the Canada-US FTA. On its own, Canada-Mexico trade and investment are not of sufficient magnitude or immediate potential to warrant bilateral negotiations. The trade statistic of $2-3 billion in two-way trade (see Table 3) may be understated as a result of transshipment through the United States, but it is of a kind and degree that can readily be handled within the context of GATT. Mexico ranked as Canada's 17th trading partner in 1988, behind Japan, the EC, the Asian NICs, the USSR and the PRC. By way of contrast, US-Mexico trade is some fifteen times larger. In short, the volume of Canadian trade with Mexico is insufficient on its own to warrant the political controversy that a bilateral negotiation would generate.

Table 3
Canada-US-Mexico Trade

	1988		1989	
	Exports	Imports	Exports	Imports
		(Thousands of Cdn. dollars)		
Canadian Trade with Mexico	489,002	1,327,726	603,098	1,698,368
Canadian Trade with the US	97,530,434	86,020,888	97,930,006	87,914,295
	1987		1988	
		(Thousands of US dollars)		
Mexican Trade with the US	20,270,785	14,569,554	23,276,890	20,633,263

Source: See Tables 5-7

In the context of a Mexico-US decision to proceed, however, the Canadian interest becomes somewhat different. Canadians should not lightly dismiss the benefits that would accrue from being part of an integrated market of 350 million people. Nor should they overlook the opening such an agreement would provide to the rest of Latin America. The division of the world into three broad trading blocs (a pan-European, East Asian and North American) may be regrettable. However, should events unfold in this manner, and it appears that they will, it may be better for Canada to be well integrated into the North American bloc than to stand alone and aloof. Secondly, by building on the 1987 FTA, Canada may find in Mexico an ally in helping to achieve some of the goals that did not prove negotiable in 1987 – such as greater access to government procurement markets and stricter controls on the application of countervailing and antidumping duties – as well as in maintaining and expanding US commitments under the FTA.

More directly, a Mexico-US agreement may well erode some of the benefits Canada gained from the FTA. It may change the equation about where footloose industries wishing to serve the North American market will decide to locate. Canada used to be the prime outlet of American foreign investment. Mexico, however, now offers its own attractions, both along the Mexico-US border for Maquiladora industries and elsewhere. While Canada would be churlish – and unsuccessful – if it sought to discourage the United States from reaching agreement with Mexico, is it in Canada's interest to be at the table ensuring that any such agreement is alert to Canadian concerns? Can Canada afford, for example, to let the US and Mexico decide which North American industries will be opened to Mexican competition and which will be sheltered? Should it allow the US and Mexico to devise rules of origin that are inimical to Canadian interests? In short, can Canada only hope to influence the future course of North American trade and investment patterns by participating or would observer status in US-Mexico negotiations suffice?

At this stage, the federal government appears to be uneasy about entering into a possibly controversial negotiation. Given the supercharged political calendar, there seems to be reluctance to add another contentious issue. Ministers are understandably apprehensive about a rerun of the 1988 election campaign. In order to overcome this nervousness, therefore, a strong case will need to be made that such an accord is in the Canadian interest and will be strongly supported by Canada's investment, export, technology and production interests. Ministers need to hear that what is at stake for Canada is direct and real rather than indirect and theoretical. They will need to be confident that there are convincing counterweights to the inevitable opposition.

That opposition is already mobilizing. The Pro-Canada Network issued a press release on June 4, 1990 trumpeting that "Canada has 'no place at the table' in free trade negotiations between the United States and Mexico." The press release noted that Canada would only be used to advance American interests and legitimize a corrupt Mexican administration. An agreement would result in the US ramming more demands for concessions down Canada's throat. Convinced that any Mexican deal would only mean "destructive competition for jobs with Mexican workers and communities," the PCN has already forged links with potential opponents in Mexico to form Common Frontiers, an organization dedicated to opposing further North American integration.[8] Council of Canadians' veteran Maude Barlow claims that a North American trade pact "would give multinationals Canada's resources, the U.S. market and Mexico's cheap labour. This is part of a plan to create one economic system that goes from Canada's North down through Central America."[9] CLC President Shirley Carr, after meeting with President Bush in his pre-Summit meetings with labour leaders, left no doubt that organized labour in Canada would oppose a North American trade pact. Lost in all the rhetoric is any concern for Mexican economic development or any alternative policies to help Canada face the emerging realities of global competition.

International trade negotiations often seek to catch up to the reality of international business. That reality is changing rapidly. We are seeing the development of truly global corporations whose decisions about what to buy and sell, where to manufacture, whose money to use and what ideas to pursue are less and less dictated by national frontiers. The issues of greatest concern to these companies and others involved in international business are not necessarily those being pursued in global trade negotiations. Private actors are finding the old trading rules inadequate and are calling for the emergence of a new order that is more in tune with this new reality. The current Uruguay Round's ambitious agenda is a response to these concerns but it remains to be seen whether there is sufficient political will to drive the negotiations to a successful conclusion. Broadly based multilateral negotiations are proving increasingly difficult and slow to respond to new challenges. Until they do, a temporary solution may lie in regional arrangements. In that context, a North American free-trade area could make eminent and constructive sense.

The chapters that follow examine the background to the rapidly changing attitude in all three countries toward further North American integration and consider the strategic implications for Canada of such integration. Chapter two sketches the geopolitical and international institutional context within which the specific concerns of Canadians must be addressed. Chapter three looks at the changes that have taken place in Mexican trade policy and the Mexican economy and compares the Mexican regime to those of Canada and the United States. The

---

8   Pro-Canada Network press release of June 4, 1990. Similar skepticism about the motives of American support for Mexico's program of economic reforms can be found in the United States. Walter Mead, writing in the *Baltimore Sun* ("Mexico Fought a Revolution on this Issue, May 8, 1990), notes: "Washington still has a touching faith in the kind of ultra-free-market, ultra-austerity programs supported by the International Monetary Fund. Raise taxes, cut social spending, pay the foreign debt, keep wages low, allow foreign companies unrestricted rights to compete in domestic markets: The doctors of the international economy prescribe these remedies to all their patients."

9   Quoted in *The Ottawa Citizen,* April 7, 1990.

next chapter turns to an examination of Canada-US-Mexico trade and investment patterns in order to assess where interests and problems for the three countries may lie. This is followed by a consideration of the various options available to Canada and an assessment of how any negotiations might be pursued. Finally, chapter six takes a close look at what would be involved in negotiating a tripartite agreement to include Mexico. Chapter seven brings the various parts of the analysis together by considering the strategic implications for Canada of the evolving North American trade agenda.

What follows does not purport to provide a detailed cost-benefit analysis of the possible impact of a North American free-trade agreement.[10] Rather, it is limited to an exploration of the events that are leading inexorably to trilateral negotiations as well as a strategic assessment of the principal issues that might arise in any such negotiations. Based on the expected results predicted by classic international trade theory from the removal of barriers to trade and investment, it assumes that all three countries would benefit to some extent – although not equally – from such an agreement. The distribution of such benefits and the necessary adjustments that would be required can only be deduced on the basis of detailed economic and sectoral analysis which would of necessity have to precede any serious negotiations.

🂠🂠🂠🂠🂠

---

[10] This kind of work is being undertaken by academic analysts in all three countries. For example, Ricardo Grinspun is heading a research consortium at York University, Len Waverman is spearheading a research program at the University of Toronto and Murray Smith of the Centre for Trade Policy and Law is working with researchers at Carleton University and El Colegio de Mexico. All three efforts aim at providing a much more detailed understanding of the trade and economic forces involved in greater North American integration. Concrete results will likely not be available for at least a year and will require that the researchers deal successfully with the formidable challenges of finding comparable data, of addressing a rapidly evolving agenda and of isolating the relevant variables. Meanwhile there is no reason why decisions should not be taken and further preparations launched.

2

The Global Context

Mexican interest either in negotiating a free-trade agreement with the United States or in a tripartite arrangement including Canada has not arisen in a vacuum. It reflects a pragmatic response by Mexico to profound changes in the multilateral trading system, the place of the United States in it and Mexico's perception of how it can best pursue a strategy to integrate its economy into the global economy. This chapter reviews the nature of some of these developments and their implications for Mexico and for the question of Mexican accession to the FTA. Many of the same considerations, of course, were fundamental to Canada's decision to negotiate its FTA with the United States.[1]

The Changing Multilateral Trading Order

For forty years, the General Agreement on Tariffs and Trade (GATT) has served as the main vehicle for promoting order in world trade. Its ability to continue in this capacity, however, has become less clear over the years. The GATT process has become increasingly slow and considerably more complex. The GATT is in urgent need of reform. Not only are the rules that deal with trade in goods beginning to show their age, but there are virtually no rules to deal with trade in

---

[1] The background to the Canadian decision to enter into bilateral negotiations with the United States can be found in volume 1 of the *Final Report* of the Royal Commission on the Economic Union and Development Prospects for Canada, the Macdonald Commission (Ottawa: Supply and Services, 1985).

services, with trade-related investment measures and with intellectual property protection. In short, the GATT rules dealing with the industries of the past are proving inadequate, and rules for the industries of the future are non-existent. The rules dealing with trade in agriculture have always been meagre and insufficient.

British economist Martin Wolf has characterized trade as an economic war and the GATT as a peace treaty among mercantilist states.[2] It is an apt metaphor. While the mercantilist states have agreed to peace, they have not fully disarmed nor are they averse to the odd skirmish. They have, for example, kept tariffs in place that serve no useful economic or even political purpose except as payment for future trade concessions. They have imposed new barriers in order to increase their bargaining leverage or to force concessions from weaker states. And they have appeased protectionist pressures, so we are told, in order to safeguard the system and provide scope for future improvement.

Enthusiasm for the idea of commercial disarmament was at its highest in the immediate post-war years when the survivors of fifteen years of depression and war agreed that there had to be a better way. That enthusiasm led to the Bretton Woods institutions (the International Monetary Fund and the World Bank) to promote international financial cooperation but was already waning when these same post-war leaders established the International Trade Organization whose rump, the GATT, remains as the only part actually implemented.[3] Enthusiasm

---

[2] See Martin Wolf, "A European Perspective," in Robert M. Stern, Philip H. Trezise and John Whalley, eds., *Perspectives on a U.S.-Canadian Free Trade Agreement* (Washington: Brookings Institution, 1987).

[3] The General Agreement on Tariffs and Trade (GATT) was adopted as an interim agreement to cover the tariff concessions negotiated among 23 countries in Geneva concurrent to the on-going negotiation of the Charter for an International Trade Organization. It is made up largely of the commercial policy chapter of the draft charter (chapter IV) and a few other articles required to give the agreement its necessary shape and form. The failure of the US Senate to ratify the Charter adopted the following year at Havana resulted in the temporary GATT functioning ever since as a substitute for the more ambitious International Trade Organization. The GATT was built out of lumber that was ready to hand in the late 1940s. It made extensive use of the language of US trade legislation, including that of the Smoot-Hawley Tariff Act of 1930, as well as the bilateral agreements negotiated under the US Reciprocal Trade Agreements Program launched in 1934. It reflected the experience and preoccupations of that era, particularly US experience and preoccupations. See William Adams Brown, *The United States and the Restoration of World Trade* (Washington: Brookings Institution, 1950) and William Diebold, Jr., *The End of the ITO* (Princeton: Princeton University Press, 1952). An essay by R. H. Snape in his *Issues in World Trade Policy: GATT at the Crossroads* (New York: St. Martin's Press, 1986) suggests the fragility of the consensus favouring commercial disarmament, and comments that even John Maynard Keynes, one of the intellectual godfathers of the postwar multilateral trade and payments system, was of two minds about the benefits of non-discrimination and freer trade.

for commercial disarmament has continued to decline ever since. One American student of the international economy has concluded that the post-war multilateral institutions have become irrelevant monuments to the past. Writes Robert Gilpin:

> A significant transformation of the postwar international economic order has occurred. The Bretton Woods system of trade liberalization, stable currencies, and expanding global economic interdependence no longer exists, and the liberal conception of international economic relations has been undermined since the mid-1970s. The spread of protectionism, upheavals in monetary and financial markets, and the evolution of divergent national economic policies among the dominant economies have eroded the foundations of the international system. Yet inertia, that powerful force in human affairs, has carried the norms and institutions of a decreasingly relevant liberal order into the 1980s.[4]

Whether relevant or not, the GATT trade relations system continues to be at the centre of modern trade negotiations. It is based on several key assumptions:

- trade policy should be non-discriminatory, as expressed in the principles of unconditional most-favoured-nation treatment and national treatment;
- the primary regulator of trade should be the highly visible mechanism of the tariff, a mechanism that affects prices, rather than other mechanisms such as quantitative restrictions;
- tariffs and other barriers to trade should be progressively reduced so that the gains from trade can be realized and economic welfare increased;
- trade results largely from the activity of private entrepreneurs rather than governments;
- governments should be allowed to impose barriers against dumped or subsidized or otherwise politically intolerable levels of imports; and
- disputes between members should be resolved through a process of consultation and negotiation, and retaliation and counter-retaliation should be avoided.

These assumptions underpin the whole agreement and if they were still broadly shared today, there would be less talk of a crisis of confidence in the GATT system. The fact of the matter is that each of these basic ideas has been undermined by exceptions, evasions and outright refusals to accept previously agreed obligations.[5]

---

4   Robert Gilpin, *The Political Economy of International Relations* (Princeton: Princeton University Press, 1987), p. 3.

5   This is the basic thesis put forward by Rodney de C. Grey in "The Decay of the Trade Relations System," in R. H. Snape, ed., *Issues in World Trade Policy: GATT at the Crossroads* (New York: St. Martin's Press, 1986).

Over the years, the system has become continually more complex in order to compensate for the failure of the more ambitious ITO to come into being, to address new problems and, most importantly, to take account of the steady decline in enthusiasm for commercial disarmament and the principles embodied in the initial peace treaty. The 35 original articles of the GATT have become encrusted with a range of ancillary or supporting arrangements, including codes, protocols, waivers, understandings, derogations, regional agreements and ad hoc institutional arrangements. Few of these have been universally accepted or applied. Many have qualified and changed the original bargain and some have even undermined progress toward the fundamental GATT objectives of freer and less discriminatory trade. Additionally, GATT has become a multi-layered instrument with various members accepting different degrees of rights and obligations.[6] GATT legal scholar John Jackson warns that GATT law, because of its studied ambiguity, backed up by an inadequate constitutional structure and flawed dispute settlement provisions, tends to be very slippery and can be bent and abused with relative impunity by its more powerful members.[7]

Despite these difficulties, GATT can lay claim to many achievements. Trade has been liberalized; tariffs have been cut; old-fashioned discriminatory quantitative restrictions have been virtually eliminated; and many potentially harmful practices have been restrained by its rules. At the same time, GATT has been unable to curb the crisis in agricultural trade, to come to grips with the new protectionism, or to address new and urgent problems arising out of the globalization of business. In many ways, therefore, the arguments about whether the GATT has been beneficial are about whether the glass is half full or half empty. Additionally, cynicism about the GATT as an institution is somewhat unfair. The system is no more than the collective will of its members. Harold Malmgren has noted that the "GATT ... is a system of balanced rights and obligations, together with a cumulation of trade agreements based on mutual concessions and on national decisions to agree, or not agree, with other nations."[8] When critics worry about the current crisis in GATT, therefore, they are really bemoaning a crisis in collective political will and leadership. The challenge is not one for GATT but for its leading members. The challenge is to come to grips with the realities of the new trade relations system and the inadequacy of mercantilist bargaining.

---

6   Gerard and Victoria Curzon, "The Multi-Tier GATT System," in Otto Hieronymi, ed., *The New Economic Nationalism* (London: MacMillan, 1980), pp. 137-147.

7   John H. Jackson, "Strengthening the International Framework of the GATT-MTN System: Reform Proposals for the new GATT Round," in Ernst-Ulrich Petersmann and Meinhard Hilf, eds., *The New GATT Round of Multilateral Trade Negotiations: Legal and Economic Problems* (Boston: Kluwer, 1989), p. 11.

8   "Threats to the Multilateral System," in William R. Cline, ed., *Trade Policy in the 1980s* (Washington: Institute for International Economics, 1983), p. 193.

The heart of the modern trade relations system is no longer the tariff and related customs administration but administered protection through such devices as antidumping and antisubsidy duties, safeguard measures and domestic policies such as supply management and subsidies.[9] Mercantilist bargaining, which seeks, through a combination of bilateral and multilateral agreements, to balance one concession against another and then extend the result to all other participants by virtue of the unconditional most-favoured-nation clause, is irrelevant when the main focus of negotiations is not specific trade barriers, but rules and procedures. The Tokyo Round of multilateral trade negotiations clearly demonstrated the problems of trying to marry the old bargaining process designed for governing trade in goods to an emerging system that goes well beyond trade in goods. The Uruguay Round is trying to expand the GATT trade relations system to a much broader agenda that seeks to recognize the changing nature of the international economy. The more than one hundred participating nations are working on an ambitious, forward-looking agenda which, if successfully addressed, would revitalize the global trading system. It remains to be seen whether the inevitable compromises between major participants will vitiate the final results.

The GATT is also gradually becoming a more legalistic as opposed to diplomatic regime. A legal regime emphasizes the adjudication of disputes based on detailed rules, procedures and precedents; a commercial diplomacy regime relies on the negotiation of unique solutions to individual problems based on general principles applied to the circumstances at hand. From the beginning, of course, GATT contained elements of both, with some members prepared to build on the legal dimension while others preferred the diplomatic approach. The subtlety of the difference between the two is captured by the contrast between American and European treatments of the GATT. American scholars have treated the GATT as largely an international legal regime while standard European texts regard GATT as primarily a diplomatic and political system.[10] These attitudinal differences have also been reflected in the contrasting approaches of the US and the EC to many GATT issues. Canadian participation tended originally to favour the diplomatic dimension but has been increasingly influenced by American academic and government commentators toward the legalistic view. Legal scholars

---

9   See Rodney de C. Grey, "The Decay of the Trade Relations System," in R. H. Snape, ed., *Issues in World Trade Policy* (New York: St. Martin's Press, 1986).

10 John H. Jackson, *World Trade and The Law of GATT* (Indianapolis: Bobbs-Merrill, 1969); Kenneth W. Dam, *The GATT: Law and International Economic Organization* (Chicago: University of Chicago Press, 1970); Gerard Curzon, *Multilateral Commercial Diplomacy: The General Agreement on Tariffs and Trade and Its Impact on National Commercial Policies and Techniques* (London: Michael Joseph, 1965); and Karin Kock, *International Trade Policy and the GATT 1947-1967* (Stockholm: Almqvist and Wiksell, 1969).

have in recent years scored some successes in convincing trade diplomats that some of the problems experienced in GATT have been the result of trying to effect legal remedies within a diplomatic regime. It is also instructive that the GATT Secretariat has over the past ten years considerably beefed up its Legal Division and that the Canadian delegation to the Uruguay Round is actively involving officials trained in the law in the preparation of position papers.[11]

Flawed Rule Making

During the Tokyo Round, participants used the old offer-request system of mercantilist bargaining to negotiate a detailed construction of rules. As a result, the industrialized countries, at the same time that they agreed to major cuts in tariffs, also adopted, with mixed results, a series of codes. For some non-tariff barriers, such as government procurement preferences, the Tokyo Round Code made an important new beginning in reducing discrimination and opening markets. Other Codes, such as the Subsidies and Countervailing Duties Agreement, provided enhanced legal sanction for the new forms of administrative protection. For smaller countries, however, one result undercut the other. For them, lower tariffs or reduced procurement preferences are meaningless if access to the larger markets can be cut off through the application of new barriers to offset dumping, subsidization or politically intolerable import levels, penalties imposed by means of highly legalistic procedures that have little to do with economic concepts.[12]

The experience of the Tokyo Round thus suggests that international rule-making may not always be in support of liberalization. As an objective, governments sought to eliminate or reduce non-tariff barriers to trade in recognition of the changing nature of the domestic trade policy regimes of the major countries. The approach adopted was to construct detailed rules and procedures rather than to continue to rely on the general principles enshrined in the GATT. The codes that were concluded adopted procedures for the uniform and transparent national application of non-tariff barriers such as licensing, standards, government procurement and antidumping and antisubsidy measures. These rules were negotiated on the basis of mercantilist bargaining – each rule perceived as a con-

---

[11] The issues involved in a reform of the GATT based on legal principles are discussed in considerable detail by a number of contributors to Ernst-Ulrich Petersmann and Meinhard Hilf, eds., *The New GATT Round of Multilateral Trade Negotiations: Legal and Economic Problems* (Boston: Kluwer, 1989), particularly John H. Jackson, "Strengthening the International Legal Framework of the GATT-MTN System: Reform Proposals for the New GATT Round," and Petersmann, "Strengthening the Domestic Legal Framework of the GATT Multilateral Trade System: Possibilities and Problems of Making GATT Rules Effective in Domestic Legal Systems."

[12] Rodney de C. Grey, *United States Trade Policy Legislation: A Canadian View* (Montreal: The Institute for Research on Public Policy, 1982).

cession to someone. It worked well for licensing, standards and government procurement where the new codes strengthened or introduced rules to reduce discrimination. It worked less well for the measures of contingency protection – antidumping and antisubsidy measures. Perversely, the result is that the scope now available for the use of these non-tariff barriers is greater than before. The Subsidies/Countervailing Duties and Antidumping Codes indirectly encouraged governments to introduce policies for which they had previously seen no need.[13] Experience with the codes to date suggests that transparency and uniformity, while they may address the virtues of stability and predictability and create employment for lawyers, are a poor substitute for the elimination of barriers.[14] Additionally, these detailed rules have tended to reinforce rather than break down existing power relationships, i.e., they are rules that benefit the trade policies of the large economies rather than those of the small economies.[15]

At the end of the Tokyo Round, US negotiators suggested that this new rule-making approach should also be used to reach international agreement in non-traditional areas of multilateral bargaining. In effect, they indicated that other changes in the trade relations system brought about by the rapid globalization of the world economy, particularly in the areas of services, investment, business travel and the protection of intellectual property, required new, comprehensive multilateral agreements. The US diagnosis of the changing global economy was generally accepted; the prescription, however, raised serious concerns. For example, the regulation of financial services in both Canada and the United States had by the mid-1980s become outdated to the point that it was acting as an impediment to beneficial growth and adjustment. Regulators scrambled to catch up with the changing realities brought about by globalization and technological

---

[13] The Canadian federal government, for example, in introducing the legislative proposals in 1980 that eventually became the *Special Import Measures Act,* argued that under existing legislation it could meet its obligations but that it could not take full advantage of its rights and thus introduced procedures to enforce trade agreement rights analogous to section 301 of US trade law and very detailed procedures to impose countervailing duties.

[14] See Rodney de C. Grey, "The General Agreement After the Tokyo Round," in John Quinn and Philip Slayton, eds., *Non-Tariff Barriers After the Tokyo Round* (Montreal: Institute for Research on Public Policy, 1982).

[15] The system of contingency protection is more likely to reward the large and powerful and harm the small and weak in at least two ways. In the first place, it takes an army of bureaucrats to make the system function and only large countries can afford such armies. Secondly, producers in small economies are more likely to find that government assistance, for example, has a direct impact on exports which then prove countervailable or run afoul of dumping laws when they meet world prices; in a large economy, the same assistance or price behaviour is likely to have an import displacement effect or be matched domestically. See Rodney de C. Grey, *United States Trade Policy Legislation: A Canadian View* (Montreal: The Institute for Research on Public Policy, 1982).

change. The need to modernize domestic law thus opened up both a threat and an opportunity – the threat of introducing discrimination where none existed before and the opportunity to develop a framework of international rules that would encourage open markets and non-discrimination in conjunction with responsible domestic regulation. It remains to be seen, however, whether detailed multilateral agreements are the best response to the threat of discrimination. Past experience suggests they can as easily codify protection as liberalization, particularly if they are constructed on the basis of mercantilist bargaining.

Changing Economic Reality: The Globalization of Business

For the business sector, the frustration lies in the growing gap between business reality and the trading system. In Mexico, Canada and the United States, developments in the Uruguay Round of trade negotiations seem hardly to be visible on business radar screens. Whereas the Canada-US negotiations were regarded with intense and immediate concern, the Uruguay Round appears to most Canadian, American and Mexican business leaders to be a remote and stylized event only barely touching their vital interests.[16] What will be decided over the next six months in Geneva and major capitals may be critical to the future evolution of the world trading system but appears rather irrelevant to those making decisions in the boardrooms of private corporations. Of course, should the system as we know it collapse as a result of protectionist unilateralism or regionalism, business would be among the first to complain.

For the private sector, it is less a question of rules than the proliferation of barriers old and new that stand in the way of rational economic decisions. Business craves stability and predictability and if the old trading order will not provide these virtues, they will be found in other ways. Those ways increasingly marginalize the old trading order. They are being found in intercorporate networking – in the negotiation of licensing and distribution agreements, in research consortia and technical joint ventures, in cross investments and joint production agreements. These techniques call for a new intergovernmental order. In a recent article in the *Wall Street Journal*, Kenichi Ohmae, managing director of McKinsey and Company in Japan, writes;

> ... the most fundamental truth of today's economic world is this: Man's ability to create and consume will not be denied by those politicians and bureaucrats who try to restrict the flows of capital, technology and information. This is a lesson not only for Eastern European communists but also for Japanese and American nationalists. (April 27, 1990)

---

16 Only 8 percent of the 635 businesses that responded to the annual survey of the Canadian Manufacturers' Association listed the GATT and the Uruguay Round as issues of concern to them in 1990. CMA member survey, 1990.

One of the basic premises of the old trading order is that goods and services have a nationality. That is increasingly not the case, particularly for the products of global corporations. Modern cars and airplanes, to take but two examples, incorporate parts sourced all over the world, involve design and engineering work by nationals of many countries, are assembled in plants on every continent, are financed by capital from a wide range of sources, and are marketed on a global basis. The Ford Probe is manufactured by Mazda and the Dodge Colt by Mitsubishi. These are neither North American nor Japanese products but global products and the companies that market them have found ingenious means of hedging against the uncertainties caused by the nationalist and mercantilist preoccupations of governments. While one group of specialists in these corporations seeks to find advantage in various national regulatory schemes, another group seeks to ensure that there are ways to neutralize them. Their apparent success should humble any politician or trade negotiator who thinks that his efforts are critical to future business decisions.[17]

Business people have long concluded that doing business in a smaller economy such as Canada or Mexico is a gamble and that the prudent course is to expand in the larger market and serve the smaller market from there. Thus for Canada and Mexico, the challenge is to find a policy framework that will make investment in Canada or Mexico less risky and more attractive. Such a framework can be found through global, bilateral or tripartite negotiations.

Macroeconomic Pressures

Finding that policy framework has been considerably complicated by the macroeconomic climate of the 1970s and 1980s. The stable exchange rates of the immediate postwar years have given way to the rapidly fluctuating exchange rates of the 1970s and 1980s. Relative budget and balance-of-payments stability has been replaced by huge deficits and surpluses.

The trade and investment climate of the 1990s will be characterized not only by a continuation of this instability but also by a world-wide shortage of private and public investment capital to meet extraordinarily high needs. In addition to normal adjustment, restructuring and expansion, capital will be needed to modernize the economies of Eastern Europe, to respond to environmental concerns and to upgrade the pace of development in the Third World. The problems will

---

17 For an arresting discussion of the growing gap between business practice and the rules of the trading system, see Sylvia Ostry, *Governments and Corporations in a Shrinking World* (New York, Council on Foreign Relations, 1990). The significance of globalization for Canadian trade and investment is discussed in Investment Canada, *The Business Implications of Globalization*, Working Paper number 1990-V, May, 1990.

be particularly acute in North America where relatively low levels of private savings and the insatiable appetites of government deficits will combine to make private capital even scarcer and more expensive.[18]

The three countries of North America are all debtor countries. Mexico faces a huge debt it is only barely able to service as a result of various international rescue efforts, including the Brady Plan. The United States became the world's number one debtor country in the 1980s while Canada continues to have one of the highest per capita debts in the world. There is no question of Canada or the United States not being able to service their debts, but both will need to run sizeable merchandise trade and even current account surpluses in the 1990s, in the absence of adequate incoming capital flows. Presently both Canada and the United States are running significant current account deficits against the rest of the world, sucking in more foreign capital and increasing total indebtedness.

These forces will place great pressures on trade and industrial policies in the 1990s and underline the need for all three economies to become more competitive vis-à-vis Europe and Japan.

Resistance to Change

However one views these challenges, the need for change and adjustment has become urgent. Efforts to modernize the GATT system to reflect the changing trade relations system, to take account of changing global business practices and to rekindle interest in liberalization, however, have met limited success. The 1982 ministerial meeting failed to reach consensus on any substantive issue. The Uruguay Round was finally launched in 1986 not because there was enthusiasm about the agenda and approach but because there was agreement that a new round would stand as a symbol of continued commitment to multilateral trade. The intervening four years have been used to develop consensus on the agenda and the negotiating parameters. Progress has been slow because the major players have approached the negotiations less as a means to advance trade liberalization and international rule-making and more as a management tool to dampen domestic protectionist pressures and reduce bilateral trade frictions. At the

---

[18] See Murray Smith, "Canada, Mexico and the United States: Pursuing Common Multilateral Interests and Exploring North American Options," paper prepared for the International Forum: Mexico's Trade Options in the Changing International Economy, Universidad Tecnologica de Mexico, Mexico City, June 11-15, 1990. Bill Cline at the same conference painted a very pessimistic picture of the macroeconomic climate within which the Uruguay Round would have to conclude and a Mexican agreement negotiated. A good general overview of the macroeconomic dimension of international trade policy can be found in Richard G. Lipsey and Murray G. Smith, *Global Imbalances and U.S. Policy Responses: A Canadian View* (Toronto: C.D. Howe Institute, 1987).

Montreal ministerial review of the negotiations in December 1988, ministers again failed to agree on any substantive issue. The difficult procedural issues were finally resolved at a meeting of senior officials in Geneva in April, 1989, thus clearing the way for substantive negotiations, but not without raising further doubts about the scope and degree of success of this round of negotiations.[19]

The United States has traditionally provided leadership in maintaining momentum toward liberalization. Today, the United States substitutes rhetoric for leadership.[20] Much of this rhetoric has a strong moral overtone, expressing anxiety about "fairness", "level playing fields" and the need for "disciplines". As Canada found out during the bilateral negotiations, it makes proposals that it cannot itself implement on a reciprocal basis.[21] It approaches international negotiations with an agenda built up from individual irritants and no longer brings comprehensive vision or substantive leadership to the table. It has yet to come to grips with the challenge to its economic leadership from Europe and Japan and with the profound changes that have taken place in the trade relations system. Until American officials adjust to these new realities, the United States will continue to have difficulty galvanizing other GATT members into forward-looking commitments that provide a balance between foreign and domestic trade policy. Notes the Bilateral Commission on the Future of United States-Mexico Relations:

> Until the U.S. addresses the fundamental financial and economic imbalances that exist, the economic system will be increasingly crisis prone, other industrial countries will be

---

[19] It is, of course, widely recognized that no major negotiation ever concludes until it has to and that the hard bargaining awaits the final push as deadlines loom. Nevertheless, by the time this stage is reached, the hard bargaining is largely procedural rather than substantive as negotiators search for the face-saving formula that will allow negotiations to conclude. That process appears to have started in Houston at the Annual Economic Summit as the leaders of the leading industrial countries faltered in their effort to make a substantive breakthrough on the issue of farm subsidies.

[20] For an American analysis of declining US leadership of the global trade relations system and the problems this poses for both the United States and the system, see Raymond Vernon and Debora L. Spar, *Beyond Globalism: Remaking American Foreign Economic Policy* (New York: The Free Press, 1989).

[21] During the FTA negotiations, for example, the US advanced positions on services from which it eventually had to retreat when Canada indicated a willingness to accept them. One of the ironies of multilateral commercial diplomacy is that the United States, which can call on a wealth of literature and insight from academic commentators, often tables the most extreme, unsophisticated and provocative position papers. These extreme positions are often used to solidify an Administration-wide position that has sufficient support in Congress to stand a chance of becoming law. In this process, much more thought is given to the short-term domestic political impact of US position papers than to their negotiability and long-term implications. It is not unusual, therefore, for American negotiators to retreat from their own proposals.

reluctant to accept U.S. leadership, international financial institutions will become less effective, trade tensions will rise, and global growth will be lowered.[22]

The European Community continues to be preoccupied with consolidating its own market. Since the Dillon Round (1961-62)[23] did not disapprove the legitimacy of the Community, it has approached multilateral negotiations defensively, ensuring that they in no way erode movement toward a unified European market supported by economic satellites in Europe, Africa and the Caribbean. Its Common Agricultural Policy (CAP) and Common External Tariff (CET), as essential building blocks holding the Community together, have been jealously guarded against inroads from multilateral negotiations. It has bound the economies of its former colonies to that of Europe in a trade and aid agreement (the Lomé Convention) that stands outside GATT. It has entered into free-trade agreements with its EFTA trading partners and used accession agreements to deny full GATT status to its Eastern European trading partners. GATT has become a less central agreement, providing international legal cover for the EC's network of special arrangements and a framework for conducting trade relations with the United States, Canada and Japan. It has adopted the US-inspired trade remedy system but without the saving grace of US attachment to transparency and due process, in effect running a Star Chamber trade law system at odds with the principles of non-discrimination.[24] Today its primary energy is directed toward the magic date of 1992 when all of Western Europe is to function as one integrated market. There are worrisome signs that many Europeans view the post-1992 integrated market as reserved for Europeans and that the Community may adopt policies to change this fear into reality. The rapidly evolving situation

---

[22] Bilateral Commission on the Future of United States-Mexico Relations, *The Challenge of Interdependence: Mexico and the United States* (New York: University Press of America, 1989), p. 49.

[23] The fifth or Dillon Round (1961-62) of multilateral trade negotiations in large measure dealt with the economic consequences for other GATT members of the 1957 Treaty of Rome establishing the Community of the Six, particularly the impact of the Common Agricultural Policy and the Common External Tariff. In a similar vein, the Tokyo Round addressed the impact of the 1973 enlargement of the Community to include the UK, Denmark and Ireland. EC spokesmen as a result take the view that they have "paid" other GATT members for the changes required by the establishment of the Community. Criticisms of the EC system today, therefore, are seen merely as ill-mannered carping about a bargain that was, with some exceptions, signed, sealed and delivered twenty years ago.

[24] On the EC as a negative force in modernizing and revitalizing the multilateral trading system, see Gardner Patterson, "The European Community as a Threat to the System," in William R. Cline, ed., *Trade Policy in the 1980s* (Washington: Institute for International Economics, 1983). On the EC system of contingency protection, see Ivo van Bael and Jean-François Bellis, *International Trade Law and Practice of the European Community – EEC Antidumping and other Trade Protection Laws* (Bicester: CCH Editions, 1985) as well as the many articles these two Brussels trade lawyers have contributed to periodicals such as the *Journal of World Trade*.

in Eastern Europe is sapping remaining European energy, as European governments and businesses find ways to integrate the markets and productive capacities of these countries into the European system.[25] European participation in the Uruguay Round reflects this defensive approach to GATT bargaining.

Japan continues to prefer bilateral accommodation to genuine international rule-making and liberalization. It has never come to terms with the essential nature of multilateralism. Its products enjoy phenomenal success on world markets while foreign exporters continue to find its market impenetrable for all but essential imports or except pursuant to bilateral arrangements. While nominally following GATT principles, Japan uses the ingenious device of administrative guidance and lax antitrust rules to deny in reality what it may accept formally. Its attitude toward multilateral bargaining is to ensure that the United States and the EC do not adopt policies harmful to Japanese interests. In short, its approach is largely dictated by export considerations. Domestic policy issues raised by its trading partners are, wherever possible, pursued bilaterally and dealt with in bilateral agreements that avoid most-favoured-nation or general non-discriminatory commitments.[26]

All three of the major players have shown a continued willingness to resolve their bilateral problems outside the parameters of the GATT.[27] The United States resolved its problem with Japan over the production of semi-conductors without reference to GATT. Conflict between the United States and the European Community over trade in beef and other farm products, including threats of retaliation and counter-retaliation, is being pursued outside the GATT. Thus both in attitude and through unilateral action and cooperative measures, the major players have undermined faith in the GATT system. As one experienced commentator has observed:

> It would be highly desirable for the governments of the two giants [the US and the EC] to be less disingenuous about the failures of the GATT, and scale back their rhetoric of attack on the meaningfulness and relevance of GATT to present-day circumstances, since

---

[25] For a balanced assessment of the implications of the drive toward a more integrated European market, see Michael Callingaert, *The 1992 Challenge from Europe: Development of the European Community's Internal Market* (Washington: National Planning Association, 1988).

[26] See the brilliant analysis of the Japanese problem by Karel van Wolferen, first in "The Japanese Problem," *Foreign Affairs,* vol. 65, no. 2 (Winter, 1987), pp. 288-303 and subsequently expanded into a full-length book, *The Enigma of Japanese Power: People and Politics in a Stateless Nation* (New York: Knopf, 1989).

[27] For a more detailed discussion of the attitudes of the major players to the multilateral trading system, see Michael M. Hart, *Canadian Economic Development and the International Trading System* (Toronto: University of Toronto Press, 1985).

they together are more responsible than the other nations for the present erosion of the multilateral disciplines.[28]

With some notable exceptions, the developing countries (LDCs) continue to be pre-occupied with the outdated concept of special and differential treatment. They insist on enjoying the rights of GATT membership without accepting its obligations and have over the years succeeded in achieving this objective. Developing countries have also found that when they become too competitive, such as in standard-technology goods like textiles, clothing and footwear, the industrialized countries have found ways to deny them their GATT rights. LDC trade and industrial policies are frankly mercantilist and are justified on the basis of a branch of development economics that has at best a fragile intellectual foundation. Leading LDC spokesmen are wary of efforts by the United States to impose disciplines on some of the more advanced LDCs and to extend GATT principles of non-discrimination to services, investment and intellectual property. Too many LDC spokesmen prefer theological discussion to pragmatic bargaining. The problems LDCs face are real and acute and require imagination and political will, not theology. While industrialized countries retain the capacity to negotiate within the GATT, the sheer preponderance of developing countries at the GATT and their predilection for posturing have, until now, made the task of determining negotiating agenda and timetables, as well as substantive discussions, enormously more difficult and made developing country participation a further drag on the system.[29]

None of these problems, even if they may be somewhat overdrawn, augur well for solid progress in the Uruguay Round. The current trade relations system is now close to fifty years old and is based on experience and concerns that are even older. Much of the system reflects the business practices and excesses of the 1930s and the negotiating experiences of that era; neither the system nor the negotiating practices reflect the reality of the 1990s. The world of the tariff and reciprocal bargaining, of trusts and currency manipulation and the other barriers and practices of the 1920s and 1930s have given way to a significant extent to problems arising from abuses of intellectual property, from franchising and li-

---

[28] Harold Malmgren, "Threats to the Multilateral System," in William R. Cline, ed., *Trade Policy in the 1980s* (Washington: Institute for International Economics, 1983), p. 199.

[29] For consideration of the intellectual deficiency of development economics and the role of the developing countries in GATT, see Deepak Lal, *The Poverty of Economic Development Economics* (Cambridge, Mass: Harvard University Press, 1985); Robert Hudec, *Developing Countries in the GATT Legal System* (London: Trade Policy Research Centre, 1988); and Martin Wolf, "Differential and More Favorable Treatment of Developing Countries and the International Trading System," *The World Bank Economic Review*, vol. 1, no. 4 (September, 1987), pp. 647-666.

censing arrangements, from the business practices of the multinational corporation, from consulting contracts and global marketing strategies.[30]

Canada, the United States and Mexico are now fully engaged in another round of multilateral trade negotiations. Despite the meager results of the Houston Economic Summit, the Uruguay Round remains potentially very significant. It continues to provide an opportunity for the trading nations of the world to come to grips with the new reality of a rapidly globalizing economy. Trying to meet this challenge on the basis of the techniques and assumptions of past multilateral negotiations, however, is unlikely to lead to the kind of results that will benefit the North American economy.

In their bilateral negotiations, Canada and, to a lesser extent, the United States made a frank assessment of current practices and appeared more willing to make serious adjustments to their domestic policies in order to meet their export objectives. This was made easier by the fact that they share a common view of many of the issues and that their two economies are organized along similar lines and are at approximately the same level of development. Such trade-offs are less likely to be made multilaterally now that the major players have moved beyond relatively innocuous barriers and have to address deeply imbedded domestic support programs. The wide disparity in economic development among the players, lack of ideological consensus and differing approaches to economic organization have made substantive results more elusive.

Over the years, as nations have become more and more interdependent and economic integration has intensified, the issues subject to international negotiation have broadened and deepened, intensifying the challenge to sovereignty. Fifty years ago, the principal issues in a trade negotiation revolved around the tariff and quantitative restrictions and the major concern was the extension of most-favoured-nation treatment.[31] In other words, negotiators concerned them-

---

[30] There have been many proposals for reform over the past few years, including two influential reports by some of the world's leading trade authorities. See Fritz Leutwiler, et. al., *Trade Policies for a Better Future: Proposals for Action* (Geneva: GATT, 1985) and Olivier Long, et al., *Public Scrutiny of Protection: Domestic Policy Transparency and Trade Liberalization* (London: Trade Policy Research Centre, 1989). Gary Banks, "Transparency, Surveillance and the GATT System," paper prepared for the fifth annual Ottawa Trade Law Conference, May 3, 1990, makes a provocative case for the kind of reforms that are needed to revitalize GATT and most of them start at home in member countries' domestic policies.

[31] See, for example, the criticism of the original GATT negotiations in 1947. Conservative leader John Bracken told the Canadian House of Commons, "Under the terms of the treaties we lose all freedom of action in directing the course of our trade.... In no circumstances can we make special arrangements to buy from those who buy from us unless we offer the same privileges to all others." House of Commons *Debates*, December 9, 1947.

selves about what happened at the border and sought to end discrimination in the way countries treated foreign goods originating in different countries. Today, negotiations cut much closer to the bone of national sovereignty and there is thus even more scope for controversy. Negotiators now deal with more than rules covering trade in goods; they are also addressing domestic policies affecting trade in services, investment, the movement of people and the protection of intellectual property. As negotiations have dug deeper into national economic life, they have tended to expose the gap between ideology and reality.[32]

The multilateral trading system is founded on the ideology of free markets pursued by private entrepreneurs; the reality is that no market is wholly free and that all economies involve a mixture of private and public enterprise. That mixture, however, varies from country to country and controversy over what is fair and what is not inevitably follows.[33] Australian trade official W. B. Carmichael has observed that:

> ... the traditional concession-swapping process in Geneva has reached an impasse. ... The increasing disorder in the international trading system has resulted from the accumulation of domestic adjustment-inhibiting actions by national governments. It is in reality a crisis in domestic policies. ... The inherent bias in the domestic policy-making process, in favour of adjustment-averting interests, has meant that successive international agreements to liberalize traditional forms of protection have generated pressure for alternative forms of assistance of an equally industry-specific nature. ... Those engaged in trade bargaining have been attempting to do so in ways which involve no visible domestic losers – that is, the least possible adjustment costs to established domestic industries. This has meant that their concessions have inevitably been confined to those trade barriers which have the least protective significance. ... At the same time, their colleagues in domestic 'industry departments' have been busy devising methods of public assistance which are no less effective than the traditional forms of protection, but which are less visible – nationally and internationally.[34]

In short, in multilateral bargaining, the emphasis by each participant has increasingly focussed on export objectives and most of the participants have been less prepared to make the necessary adjustments in their domestic policies to make the system work. The result has been deadlock. In the Canada-US bilateral nego-

---

[32] See Michael M. Hart, "The Mercantilist's Lament: National Treatment and Modern Trade Negotiations," *Journal of World Trade Law*, vol 21 (1987), pp. 38-61.

[33] Writes Stanley Marcuss, "The disagreements that currently exist regarding what to do about domestic subsidies or how to treat them are grounded in fundamentally complex and different views about the proper role government should play in society and in the marketplace." "Understanding Direct and Indirect Subsidies: Are the Problems Negotiable or Incurable?" in Don Wallace, Jr., Frank J. Loftus and Van C. Krikorian, *Interface Three: Legal Treatment of Domestic Subsidies* (Washington: The International Law Institute, 1984), p. 51.

[34] W. B. Carmichael, "National Interests and International Trade Negotiations," *The World Economy*, vol. 10 (1987), pp. 342 and 346-7.

tiations, while the negotiators on each side proceeded initially on the basis of traditional objectives, each side recognized, with some important exceptions, the need for meaningful adjustments in their domestic policies. The result was a more far-reaching agreement than appears possible multilaterally.

The Appeal of Regionalism

For many countries, regional agreements have developed as a substitute for multilateral negotiations. They provide some of the benefits of broad, multilateral agreements but may involve less painful adjustment costs and, particularly when they involve neighbours with shared values and attitudes, prove easier to negotiate. Notes Peter Morici:

> Among smaller groups of countries having much in common in terms of their development characteristics, economic and legal institutions, and political culture, the balance of economic benefits and adjustments costs are more predictable and controllable, and the technical problems of policy harmonization coincident with many nontariff issues are more manageable than in the broader GATT context. Moreover, the regional expansion of trade within Europe, North America, and East and Southeast Asia avoids the inevitable conflicts between the EC, the United States and Japan regarding the appropriate scope of market-responsive government policies to achieve social goals and assist industry in spreading and brokering risks.[35]

Canada, the United States and Mexico are relative newcomers to the regionalization of trade relations.[36] With the exception of the 1965 Autopact and the special provisions covering trade in defence products, North America has eschewed regional arrangements. The United States and Canada have relied almost exclusively on GATT while Mexico has had very few arrangements of any kind.

This has not been the case in other regions. From the beginning, European politicians pursued a vigorous regional program starting with the European Coal and Steel Community of 1954 through to the current European Community of 12 countries to which are attached through other arrangements most of the other countries of Western Europe, as well as former colonies in Africa, the Pacific and the Caribbean. Over the next few years, we are likely to see Eastern Europe become firmly tied to the EC through a new series of arrangements. The countries

---

35 Peter Morici, "Regionalism in the International Trading System and Mexico-U.S. Relations," paper prepared for the International Forum: Mexico's Trade Options in the Changing International Economy, Universidad Tecnologica de Mexico, Mexico City, June 11-15, 1990, p. 11.

36 A full list of regional arrangements notified to GATT appear in an annex to Jeffrey Schott, ed., *Free Trade Areas and U.S. Trade Policy* (Washington: Institute for International Economics, 1988), pp. 376-381.

of Asia, Africa and Latin America have also experimented with various regional arrangements.

These regional agreements have become attractive despite the fact that multi-lateral agreements are superior from both an economic and a political perspec-tive. Multilateral agreements, because they prevent discrimination among sour-ces, allow buyers to source their goods from the lowest-cost producers. Within a single, non-discriminatory system, transaction costs are relatively low, again pro-moting efficiency. Politically, because unconditional multilateralism and non-discrimination lead to equality of treatment, friction and disputes are minimized and the probability of trade being used as a weapon of foreign policy is re-duced.[37]

But in a world of political and economic insecurity where global arrange-ments are difficult to negotiate, the political and economic arguments favouring multilateralism rarely prevail against the more persuasive arguments of vested interests. American geopolitical impulses of the 1940s and 1950s, for example, have increasingly become subordinated to the particularism of special interests as US hegemony gave way to shared responsibility. Regionalism has, as a result, emerged as a pragmatic, second-best solution. Notes Sidney Weintraub:

> The real world systemic issue is whether regionalism can exist alongside multilateralism and not whether regionalism can be exorcised. Even this formulation is not precise enough, because the two now do coexist. Can regionalism in North America involving Mexico as well as Canada in preferential relations with the United States, coexist harmoniously with the multilateral GATT system? This is the question raised by the prospective Mexico-U.S. agreement. The trade policy task is less to deplore what is happening, than to prevent the reality that is taking place from becoming disaster.[38]

It is within this context that Mexican business and political leaders are re-ex-amining how best to define and manage their relationship with the United States. Their concerns and pre-occupations should be familiar to many Canadians. There are many parallels between the current Mexican debate and the debate in Canada in the 1980s. Canadians also decided that they needed to redefine their relation-

---

[37] These and other arguments are deployed in a spirited defense of multilateralism by C. Michael Aho in "More Bilateral Trade Agreements Would be a Blunder: What the New President Should Do," *Cornell International Law Journal,* vol. 22, no. 1 (Winter, 1989), pp. 25-38. An equally interesting and more detailed criticism of regionalism from an Australian per-spective can be found in Andrew Stoeckel, David Pearce and Gary Banks, *Western Trade Blocs: Game, Set or Match for Asia-Pacific and the World Economy* (Canberra: Centre for International Economics, 1990).

[38] See Sidney Weintraub, "The North American Free Trade Debate," paper prepared for the International Forum: Mexico's Trade Options in the Changing International Economy, Universidad Tecnologica de Mexico, Mexico City, June 11-15, 1990, pp. 22-23.

ship to the United States. More open and more secure access to the market with which we conducted three-quarters or more of our international business was considered critical to underwriting domestic industrial restructuring. The GATT was considered to be unable to achieve that objective either quickly enough or thoroughly enough. Closer economic relations with the United States, however, raised profound concerns and strident opposition. While the FTA is now law, support for its provisions remains less than universal. Thus, while the economic reasons for a tripartite arrangement involving Mexico may be persuasive, the politics of such a development are less certain. A clearer understanding of the road Mexico has travelled, however, may help place the issue into better perspective.

❧❧❧❧❧

3

The North American Trade Regime

Just as growing disillusionment with the multilateral trading order has made consideration of a North American accord respectable in Canada, the United States and Mexico, growing convergence in the trade regimes of the three countries of North America has made such an accord both feasible and desirable. The United States, which for long had the most open and stable regime, has gradually turned inward and become less convinced about its past policies, stepping up anxiety in Canada and Mexico about the security of their access to the US market. At the same time Canada has gradually turned its back on the mercantilism of its National Policy and, as a result of the free-trade agreement, made a major commitment to a more outward-looking and market-oriented regime. Mexico has unilaterally reversed more than a century of protectionism and dramatically opened its market to foreign competition. As a result of these changes, the trade regimes of all three countries are now sufficiently similar to permit consideration of the negotiation of a trilateral accord.

Evolution of Mexican Trade Policy and the Mexican Economy

Although Mexico is unlike Canada in most respects, the two countries do share a long history of trying to live in harmony with but distinct from the United States.

That is not an easy task. The United States from its earliest beginnings showed it-self to be extremely self-confident, convinced of its manifest destiny. On the basis of a rapidly expanding and wealthy continental economy, it exported not only its abundance of agricultural, resource and manufactured products, but also its cul-tural values and political ethos. Its neighbours to the north and south were not always sure they wanted to import these latter qualities and shied away from entanglements that might compromise indigenous values and priorities. Dating back to the nineteenth century, therefore, there has always been tension between economic objectives and other values pursued in bilateral relations with the United States.[1]

Over the past forty years, Canada has found that the multilateral system al-lowed it to have the best of both worlds. It could negotiate trade liberalization agreements with the United States but within a framework that provided coun-terweights to the dominance of the United States. Mexico chose a different path to maintain its distance from the United States. With the brief exception of a 1942 bilateral agreement under the Reciprocal Trade Agreements Program, Mexico avoided any economic entanglements with the United States. It stood largely apart from the developments leading to the postwar multilateral trade and pay-ments system. It did not join the GATT. Rather, it pursued a policy of industrial-ization through import substitution.[2] While Mexico and the United States ex-tended MFN treatment to each other, there was no treaty basis for this nor did it matter much: throughout most of the postwar years, foreign trade constituted less than ten percent of Mexico's GDP.[3]

---

[1]   See Seymour Martin Lipsett, *Continental Divide: The Values and Institutions of the United States and Canada* (Toronto: C.D. Howe Institute, 1989) and Sidney Weintraub, *Marriage of Convenience: Relations between Mexico and the United States* (Washington: 1990).

[2]   Mexico was not a member of the preparatory committee charged with developing a charter for an International Trade Organization (ITO) and which, concurrently, negotiated the General Agreement on Tariffs and Trade (GATT) as an interim agreement in 1947. Mexico was an active participant at the Havana Conference which sought to establish the ITO but was dissatisfied with the result and consequently declined to join the GATT. Instead, it chose to follow the policies recommended for all of Latin America by the Economic Commission for Latin America, ECLA, based on the ideas of Raoul Prebisch that the terms of trade for un-derdeveloped countries were unequal, making reliance on trade against their interests; only by building from within through the development of import substitution industries would such countries eventually prosper.

[3]   Mexico's ratio of combined exports and imports to GDP rose from under 10 percent in 1970 to almost 40 percent in 1987. See Bilateral Commission on the Future of United States-Mexico Relations, *The Challenge of Interdependence: Mexico and the United States* (New York: University Press of America, 1989), p. 59.

Throughout the 1970s, Mexico benefitted from the rapid increase in energy prices and as a result, borrowed heavily on international markets both to finance economic development and to maintain expensive domestic support programs. Flush with oil money, it could afford to maintain its ruinously costly import substitution policy. In the 1970s, the administrations of Luis Echeverria Alvarez (1971-76) and José Lopez Portillo (1977-82) felt sufficiently confident to flirt with a more outward-looking foreign policy and Mexico became one of the more active voices within the group of 77, the group of developing countries seeking the establishment of a New International Economic Order. This was an opening to the South rather than the North. Strident anti-American rhetoric was part of the regular political vocabulary of the Echeverria and Portillo administrations.[4]

Accession to GATT was to be one of the main vehicles of Mexico's more open orientation. Mexico participated in the Tokyo Round of GATT negotiations and gained significant tariff concessions from other participants. In 1979 it negotiated a protocol of accession to GATT.[5] In March of 1980, however, President Portillo changed his mind. Growing opposition to his foreign entanglements as well as the degree of adjustment that GATT membership would entail doomed the initiative. The critics of GATT membership scored heavily by emphasizing that the GATT was a creature of the United States and GATT membership would result in increased American influence on Mexican life. Despite strong support in his cabinet for GATT membership, Portillo withdrew Mexico's application and decided to maintain its highly interventionist trade and economic regime.[6]

Two years later the roof fell in. The Administration of Miguel de la Madrid (1983-88) not only had to weather a drastic fall in oil prices, but also a worldwide depression. Mexico found itself saddled with a debt load that it could not service, a manufacturing sector that could not compete, a bloated public sector that sucked up much needed investment capital and a business sector that had lost confidence in Mexico's ability to recover. Millions of dollars of private capital fled to safer havens. The value of the peso plummeted and inflation soared. The standard of living for most ordinary Mexicans was cut in half. Mexico, which for years had prided itself on being one of the most stable Latin American

---

4   See Sidney Weintraub, *Marriage of Convenience: Relations between Mexico and the United States* (Washington: 1990). Mexican trade policies in the 1960s and 1970s are described in Nisso Bucay and Eduardo Perez Motta, "Mexico," chapter 6 in John Whalley, ed., *Dealing with the North: Developing Countries and the Global Trading System* (London: Centre for the Study of International Economic Relations, 1987).

5   The report of the Working Party can be found at page 238, GATT, *Basic Instruments and Selected Documents*, vol. 26 (Geneva, 1981).

6   Dale Story, "Trade Politics and the Third World: A Case Study of the Mexican GATT Decision," *International Organization*, vol. 36, no. 4 (1982).

economies, had joined the club of problem countries. The IMF and international bankers were quick to point the way to recovery: an end to the import substitution strategy, a reduction in the size of the public sector, and an end to other interventionist policies. Mexican leaders were faced with a stark choice: open up and modernize the economy in order to earn foreign exchange to service the debt or continue along the old path and repudiate the debt.[7]

At first tentatively and then with increasing confidence, de la Madrid and his cabinet showed themselves willing to follow the advice of the international bankers. In 1985 Mexico did what few democracies have been prepared to do: it unilaterally declared commercial disarmament by initiating a massive reform of its trade regime and re-applying for GATT membership. World Bank President Barber Conable characterized Mexico's program as "one of the most ambitious, courageous and determined programs of economic reform and institutional change recently undertaken in any country."[8] The report of the 1986 GATT Working Party[9] told the tale of years of excess. Unlike the 1979 report which suggested a militantly defiant Mexico insisting on special and differential treatment as a developing country, the 1986 report shows a determined Mexico prepared to accept the necessary pain and to take the necessary steps to bring its regime into compliance with GATT obligations. While insisting on its rights as a developing country, it also took pride in being able to meet many of GATT's requirements. Noted two Mexican economists:

> Mexico entered the GATT in 1986 under less favorable conditions than those obtained in 1979, and in contrast to 1979 there was little public debate. The entry into GATT was seen as part of the government's general economic policy that sought the structural adjustment of the productive sector toward an export-oriented strategy. It is interesting to note that the terms of the debate in 1986 were mainly technical as the only skepticism regarding the decision concerned whether it was necessary to enter the GATT in order to implement a policy of structural adjustment.[10]

The 1986 GATT report also indicates how complex and counterproductive the old regime had become. The Mexican version of the welfare state brought in its train massive inefficiency and dislocation of resources. Productivity growth had

---

[7] See Sidney Weintraub, "Mexican Foreign Trade: Policies, Results and Implications," in *Mexican Trade Policy and the North American Community* (Washington: Center for Strategic and International Studies, 1988).

[8] Quoted in *The Financial Post,* March 21, 1990, p. 12.

[9] GATT, *Basic Instruments and Selected Documents,* vol. 33 (Geneva, 1987), at p. 56.

[10] Nisso Bucay and Eduardo Perez Motta, "Trade Negotiation Strategy for Mexico," in John Whalley, ed., *The Small Among the Big* (London: Center for the Study of International Economic Relations, 1988). Perez Motta is now part of Commerce Secretary Jaime Serra's team, responsible for GATT affairs.

come to a virtual standstill in the previous decade. In order to shield Mexico from international competition, the Mexican government had introduced a bewildering array of tariffs, duties, drawbacks, export and tax incentives, dual exchange rates, price controls, licensing schemes, user fees, subsidies, preferences, official prices and other import restricting and export enhancing measures. Tariffs ranged from 0 to 100 percent with rates for individual items changing as circumstances warranted. Almost all imports required a prior import authorization or license, to which access was neither certain nor transparent. Foreign investment was heavily restricted, often requiring Mexican participation; most foreign investors decided not to bother. This was a National Policy with a vengeance.

The program of unilateral reform introduced in July of 1985 hacked away mercilessly at the layers of restrictions. Applied tariff rates were cut in half and then in half again. By the end of 1987, a ceiling of 20 percent had been placed on all tariffs, with many being applied at 5, 10 and 15 percent. The trade-weighted impact of the tariff is now down to around 10 percent, in line with that of Canada.[11] Licences have been eliminated for the majority of goods; again, by 1990, only a small proportion of products (less than one-fifth of actual imports) still requires prior import authorization. Quantitative restrictions have been eliminated for all but the most sensitive sectors – agriculture, oil and petrochemicals, motor vehicles, pharmaceuticals, footwear and electronic equipment. Official prices for customs valuation purposes have been abolished. Import fees and formalities have been standardized. Export incentives have been reduced. Investment restrictions have been loosened – many sectors are now open to 100 percent foreign participation. Money-losing public enterprises have been sold to private entrepreneurs (801 of 1115 public enterprises have been or are being sold, including Mexico's two airlines).[12] Within five years, Mexico's trade regime has moved

---

[11] Estimates of the trade-weighted impact of Mexico's tariff differ. The USITC estimates that it moved from a high of 28.5 percent in December, 1985 to 11 percent by May of 1988 (*Review of Trade and Investment Liberalization Measures by Mexico and Prospect for Future United States-Mexican Relations*, Publication 2275 of April, 1990, p. 4-3). Jeffrey Schott posits that it has moved down further to 6.2 percent ("A Strategy for Mexican Trade Policy in the 1990s," paper prepared for the International Forum: Mexico's Trade Options in the Changing International Economy, Universidad Tecnologica de Mexico, Mexico City, June 11-15, 1990, p. 1). Sidney Weintraub at the same conference suggested the figure was now about 9 percent.

[12] The most detailed account of the reforms in Mexico's trade and investment policies can be found in a report prepared by the US International Trade Commission, *Review of Trade and Investment Liberalization Measures by Mexico and Prospect for Future United States-Mexican Relations*, Publication 2275 of April, 1990. A less detailed version can be found in Sidney Weintraub, "Mexican Foreign Trade: Polices, Results and Implications," in *Mexican Trade Policy and the North American Community* (Washington: Center for Strategic and International Studies, 1988).

from an extremely restrictive and interventionist regime typical of many developing countries to a regime that is comparable to that of many industrialized countries. The prestigious World Economic Forum recently concluded that "Mexico has evolved from being one of the most closed economies in the world only a few years ago to one of the most open today."[13]

Mexico is now firmly on the road toward becoming a market-oriented, open economy with a disciplined public sector and solid prospects for growth. It is trying to imitate the successful policies pursued earlier by the Asian NICs and the southern tier of Europe in developing a modern mixed economy.[14] The public sector is no longer seen as the primary vehicle for economic development and government policy is encouraging more productive use of foreign and domestic private capital. The public share of gross fixed investment declined from a high of 46.5 percent in 1982 to 29.6 percent by the end of 1988.[15]

Table 4
Trade Reforms Undertaken by Mexico, 1985-89
(in percent)

	1985		1986		1987		1988	1989
	June	Dec.	June	Dec.	June	Dec.	May	March[3]
Items covered by import license[1]	92.2	47.1	46.9	39.8	35.8	25.4	23.2	22.3
Items covered by reference prices[1]	18.7	25.4	19.6	18.7	13.4	0.6	0.0	0.0
Maximum tariff	100.0	100.0	45.0	45.0	40.0	20.0	20.0	20.0
Average tariff rate[2]	23.5	28.5	24.0	24.5	22.7	11.8	11.0	12.6

1. with respect to tradable output
2. trade-weighted average tariff
3. Preliminary figures
    Source: USITC Publication 2275

---

[13] World Economic Forum, *The Competitiveness of the Mexican Economy: A Progress Report*, p. 9.

[14] There is broad consensus within the GATT-based trade relations system that no government can fundamentally alter the forces of comparative advantage and market discipline. Events in Mexico itself bear out this contention. This does not translate, however, into broad consensus that governments have no role to play in their domestic economies. On the contrary, the US is virtually isolated in its ideological commitment to market forces and the evils of government intervention, an ideology it honours more in the breach than in the observance. The Mexican trade regime of both private and public enterprise, therefore, fits fully into the GATT system. A good account of the tension between US ideology and practice can be found in I. M. Destler, *American Trade Politics: System Under Stress* (Washington: Institute for International Economics, 1986).

[15] Banco de Mexico figures reproduced in a handbook prepared by SECOFI (Ministry of Commerce and Industrial Development).

The reforms paid dramatic and immediate dividends. Exports doubled in the first two years while imports soared. Real per capita consumption showed a 6.4 percent increase in 1987 followed by a 25.3 percent increase in 1988 – after an average yearly decline of 2 percent the previous five years.[16] New investment by Mexican and foreign investors took off at an unprecedented rate. Maquiladora industries in northern Mexico mushroomed to take advantage of low-cost labour and in-bond processing rules as well as the US outward-processing program.[17] Recent economic statistics underscore the impact of the reforms: inflation down from 160 percent two years ago to under 20 percent today; real GDP, after stagnating and then decreasing, rose 1.5 percent in 1987, 1.1 percent in 1988 and 3.0 percent in 1989; the government fiscal deficit decreased from 16 percent of GDP in 1987 to 6 percent in 1989; official and private foreign debt reduced from US$107.4 billion in 1987 to US$96.3 billion by the middle of 1989; labour productivity, after decreasing steadily in the first half of the 1980s, rose 8.4 percent in 1987 and 34.9 percent in 1988; and new foreign investment rose from $4.6 billion in 1982-85 to almost $12 billion in 1986-89. Most important of all, Mexicans again showed confidence in their own economy: in 1989 alone, Mexicans brought home and invested $2.5 billion.[18]

Table 5
Mexican Harmonized Import Tariff System
May 31, 1989

Total number of current tariff items	11,949	Total number of items that require	
Prohibited	17	import license	326
Duty-free	216	Duty-free	30
5 percent duty	92	5 percent duty	9
10-percent duty	6,006	10-percent duty	178
15-percent duty	3,251	15-percent duty	13
20-percent duty	2,367	20-percent duty	96

Source: USITC Publication 2275

---

16 World Economic Forum, *The Competitiveness of the Mexican Economy: A Progress Report*, p. 9.

17 The Mexican Maquiladora or "in-bond" industries were set up to take advantage of US legislation relating to foreign production using US inputs. Maquilas import US components duty free and in-bond into Mexico and use these in the assembly and further manufacturing of upstream products which are then exported back to the United States. US importers need to pay duty only on the value-added in Mexico. In the absence of a similar program in Canada, few Canadian companies have invested in maquilas. See below for the significance of the Maquiladora program for Mexican development.

18 Data extracted from World Economic Forum, *The Competitiveness of the Mexican Economy: A Progress Report*, and US International Trade Commission, *Review of Trade and Investment Liberalization Measures by Mexico and Prospect for Future United States-Mexican Relations*, Publication 2275 of April, 1990.

But new problems also arose. As Mexican companies penetrated the American market with new zeal, they found themselves caught in US process protectionism: antidumping and countervailing duties multiplied. Between 1980 and 1986, Mexico was caught up in 26 countervailing duty investigations, 19 of which led to restrictive actions of one kind or another.[19] Access to other markets proved similarly unreliable. For Mexican manufacturers, priorities had changed making concern about access real for the first time. Exports, rather than the domestic market, were now to provide the engine for growth. And more than anything else, the American market, as the only realistic market in the short to medium term, became the main focus of attention.[20]

In order to improve access to Mexico's most important market, negotiations were initiated with the United States to satisfy some of the more egregious American complaints about Mexican practices and to gain more secure access in return. The results included a 1985 agreement on subsidies which entitled Mexican products to the injury test under US countervailing duty procedures; a 1987 framework agreement involving a work program leading to possible further concessions by both sides; and a 1989 Understanding Regarding Trade and Investment Talks, further expanding a work program aimed at more extensive agreements. These bilateral discussions built mutual confidence and provided each side with valuable negotiating experience while scoring small but important successes.[21] But the thorny issue of process protectionism – antidumping and countervailing duties and safeguards – has remained impermeable to negotiations and maintained Mexican anxiety about the security of its access to the United States market.

To consolidate its reforms, Mexico agreed to bind its new trade regime in the GATT. A business-like Working Party made short work of the protocol of accession and on August 24, 1986 the Contracting Parties welcomed Mexico as its 92nd member. Mexico agreed to bind its tariffs at 50 percent and to continue its

---

[19] See Table 4.6 in Sidney Weintraub, *A Marriage of Convenience: Relations Between Mexico and the United States* (New York: Oxford University Press, 1990), pp. 81-82.

[20] See Sidney Weintraub, "The North American Free Trade Debate," paper prepared for the International Forum: Mexico's Trade Options in the Changing International Economy, Universidad Tecnologica de Mexico, Mexico City, June 11-15, 1990, p. 2. See also Luis Rubio, "The Changing Role of the Private Sector," in Susan Kaufman Purcell, *Mexico in Transition: Implications for U.S. Policy* (New York: Council on Foreign Relations, 1988), pp. 31-42.

[21] Jeffrey Schott in "A Strategy for Mexican Trade Policy in the 1990s," paper prepared for the International Forum: Mexico's Trade Options in the Changing International Economy, Universidad Tecnologica de Mexico, Mexico City, June 11-15, 1990, p. 4 notes how agreements on trade in steel and textiles have satisfied both Mexican and American preoccupations. The Mexicans will continue to restrain exports of steel and textiles but in return have gained larger quotas than might otherwise have been imposed on them.

program of reform. It agreed to join the GATT Antidumping, Licensing, Standards and Valuation Agreements and bring its regime into line with these codes. To underscore that it had become a full member of the club, however, Mexico emphasized that future reforms would require some reciprocity. Its political capacity for unilateralism was nearing exhaustion. Additionally, it stressed that its protocol of accession would require similar provisions to the original protocol of 1947, i.e., it would not be able to bring all of its laws into conformity with GATT but would strive to make gradual reforms.[22] True to that promise, Mexican officials have played an active and constructive role in the Uruguay Round of GATT negotiations by tabling innovative proposals and actively promoting various ways to resolve issues, including on safeguards, trade-related intellectual property and investment issues, and services. Unlike the Mexico of a decade ago, it has taken a resolutely independent line, refusing to be drawn into positions of LDC solidarity that do not coincide with Mexico's interests.

But Mexico is also discovering that GATT participation has its limits. While it will gain some improvement in access to the markets of the US, EC and Japan, these will in no way match the extent to which Mexico has opened its markets to US, EC and Japanese goods. Mexico's voice is but one of many. The brave ideas discussed early in the Round are being modified in the light of negotiating realities as the Round draws to a conclusion. Issues of greatest import to Mexico are no longer at the top of the priority list. Joining the GATT in 1986 was a major step involving significant political risk. It is successfully underwriting domestic economic reform. But in order to consolidate that reform, many Mexicans will expect it to pay dividends in terms of improved access to foreign markets and improved rules for the conduct of trade. To maintain the momentum of domestic reform, therefore, Mexicans are considering whether GATT negotiations are enough. The critical factor in this equation will be the extent to which the Uruguay Round of multilateral trade negotiations opens up the American market and contains process protectionism in the United States and Europe. The Mexican private sector had concluded by late 1989 that the Uruguay Round would not achieve this objective; Mexican politicians and officials agreed by the middle of 1990.

---

22 The report of the Working Party can be found in GATT, *Basic Instruments and Selected Documents*, vol. 33 (Geneva, 1987), at p. 56. The GATT Protocol of Provisional Accession was the vehicle used in 1947 to bring the General Agreement into effect until the more comprehensive negotiations on the Havana Charter concluded. The Protocol required that parts I and III of the GATT be brought into force fully and part II, containing many of the key articles, only insofar as it was not inconsistent with existing legislation. In this way, the US administration was able to bring the GATT into effect without congressional approval and without overstepping its negotiating authority.

An important factor in Mexican thinking was the successful conclusion of the Canada-US FTA in 1987. In the following two years, Mexican business, government and academic leaders blew hot and cold on the issue but finally concluded that they had to achieve access to the US equivalent to that gained by Canada.[23]

The combined effect of a changing domestic economy, the need for greater and more secure access to its principal foreign market, the United States, realization of the inability of the GATT directly and immediately to address Mexican trade policy concerns, and increasing process protectionism in the United States thus fuelled the debate in Mexico about the future direction of its trade policy and relations with the United States. The bilateral or regional option took on an urgency that no one would have foreseen only a few years ago. Originally confined to academics and other specialists, it has gradually expanded to business leaders and then to politicians and government officials. The next step will be to determine whether an agreement responsive to Mexican interests is negotiable.

Canada: Slow Retreat from the National Policy

For Canada, the 1980s also marked a revolution. Canada finally abandoned the twin objectives of the National Policy[24] – the maintenance of high levels of protection for the domestic manufacturing sector while seeking more open access to foreign markets for Canada's resources – and adopted policies aimed at making the manufacturing sector more competitive on a global basis through

---

23 See Gerardo Bueno, "A Mexican View," in William Diebold, Jr., ed., *Bilateralism, Multilateralism and Canada in U.S. Trade Policy* (New York: Council on Foreign Relations, 1988) and Sidney Weintraub, "The Impact of the Agreement [the Canada-US FTA] on Mexico" in Peter Morici, ed., *Making Free Trade Work* (New York: Council on Foreign Relations, 1990).

24 The National Policy was introduced in 1879 by the Conservative Government of Sir John A. Macdonald in part as a response to US indifference to renewing the Reciprocity Agreement of 1854. The National Policy sought to induce economic development and manufacturing in Canada through a combination of high tariffs, infrastructure development and immigration policies. The trade policy elements were continually adjusted over the years but until the 1950s, Canada never wavered from the twin objectives of developing import-substitution manufacturing through high levels of protection while seeking access to foreign markets for Canada's abundance of resource products. The Machinery Program was a good example. It provided for low tariffs for imported machinery until such time as a Canadian manufacturer offered equivalent machinery when a higher rate would go into effect. The decision whether or not a particular machine was made in Canada offered the government wide scope to influence trade and industrial development decisions and exasperated Canada's trading partners. Through seven rounds of GATT negotiations, Canada managed to maintain a higher level of protection for industrial products than other OECD countries. A more detailed examination of the National Policy and its influence on subsequent Canadian trade policy and practice will be found in Michael Hart, *From Colonialism to Interdependence: The Historical Foundations of Modern Canadian Trade Policy* (Ottawa: Centre for Trade Policy and Law, forthcoming).

freer trade. The Canada-US free-trade agreement was a central part of that policy stance. It reflected a pragmatic assessment that multilateral negotiations would not provide a sufficient guarantee for the significant restructuring that Canadian manufacturers needed to undertake. Indeed, multilateral bargaining had made it too easy for Canada to avoid adjustment.[25]

In the 1960s and 1970s Canada was often accused of being one of the more adept exploiters of multilateral mercantilist bargaining – it was called the quintessential free rider, whether by accident or design. In a multilateral negotiation, any concessions negotiated between two states are made available to all other members. As a result, there develops a hierarchy in the negotiating process. Market power remains the basic prerequisite to gaining concessions – the more concessions one has to offer, the more concessions one is likely to gain. Thus, particularly as long as the tariff was the main instrument of protection, the major deals were struck among European countries and between them and the United States. When Europe began to bargain as one and Japan became a major economic power, the negotiations became three-cornered. By the time the Big Three got to Canada, only the United States had much interest. Canada thus benefitted from the bargains struck by the Big Three but made significant concessions of its own only in its bilateral bargaining with the United States.

One side effect of this fact of multilateral life was that the multilateral system perversely reinforced the pull of geography, a pull which Canadians were told could only be resisted through multilateral bargaining. Efforts in the mid-1970s to reverse the trend through framework agreements with the EC and Japan had little economic effect because they had no contractual teeth to them. A second side effect was that much Canadian energy was always devoted to ensuring that the Big Three reached a bargain among themselves which would be favourable to Canadian interests but for which Canada would have to pay a minimum in concessions of its own. It was a pragmatic response to an inescapable fact of multilateral life.[26]

---

25 The latest and most complete description of Canadian trade policy will be found in GATT, *Trade Policy Review 1990: Canada* (Geneva: GATT, forthcoming).

26 Throughout the 1970s and into the 1980s, one of the most frequently deployed arguments in Canada against bargaining with the United States outside the GATT was that the multilateral system acted as a counterweight to the disparity in power between the two countries and helped to arrest the geographic drift toward increasing dependence on the US market. In fact, the multilateral system reinforced the pull of geography and increased Canadian dependence on the United States. For the "orthodox" foreign policy view, see Mitchell Sharp, "Canada-U.S. Relations: Options for the Future," *International Perspectives,* Special Issue, Autumn, 1972 and Department of External Affairs, *A Review of Canadian Trade Policy* (Ottawa: Supply and Services, 1983). A wittier and more considered view can be found in John W. Holmes, *Life With Uncle: The Canadian-American Relationship* (Toronto: University of Toronto Press, 1981).

The state of domestic Canadian trade policy after seven rounds of multilateral bargaining and before implementation of the free-trade agreement with the United States illustrated the results of this strategy. Canada had the highest average MFN tariff levels among industrialized countries. Canada relied more on the

Chart 1
Canadian and US Levels of Tariff Protection in 1987

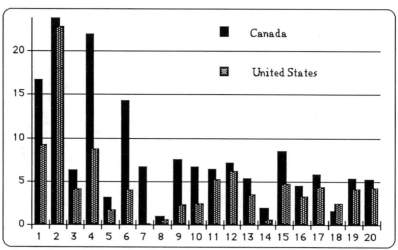

Source: External Affairs, *Canadian Trade Negotiations: Introduction, Selected Documents and Further Reading*, p. 48.

1.	Textiles	11.	Nonmetal mineral products
2.	Wearing apparel	12.	Glass and glass products
3.	Leather products	13.	Iron and steel
4.	Footwear	14.	Nonferrous metals
5.	Wood products	15.	Metal products
6.	Furniture and fixtures	16.	Nonelectrical machinery
7.	Paper and paper products	17.	Electrical machinery
8.	Printing and publishing	18.	Transportation equipment
9.	Chemicals	19.	Miscellaneous manufactures
10.	Rubber products	20.	All industries

One of the myths of this aspect of modern Canadian foreign policy is that its intellectual roots can be found in the thoughts and actions of the "giants" of the past – Lester Pearson, Norman Robertson, John Deutsch and others who, so the myth goes, were attracted to the multilateral system as a counterweight to the power of the United States. That myth is debunked in the context of the secret 1947-48 trade negotiations with the United States in Michael Hart, "Almost But Not Quite: the 1947-48 Bilateral Canada-US Negotiations," *American Review of Canadian Studies*, vol. XIX, Spring 1989, pp. 25-58.

tariff and tariff-related programs for protection than any other member of the OECD. Canadians proudly proclaimed that prior to the FTA 80 percent of trade with the United States was free, failing to mention that a lot more trade could have taken place if 80 percent of tariff rates had been free.[27] Most Canadian exports were concentrated in resources at relatively low levels of processing or in automotive products benefitting from the bilateral Autopact.[28] The domestic manufacturing industry was small, fragmented and inefficient, concentrating on supplying the domestic market, a state of affairs encouraged by the high levels of both Canadian and US tariff protection for fully processed goods. All that will change as a result of the FTA, but not overnight. It will require an alert business community to take advantage of new opportunities as well as some painful adjustment.[29]

Like other GATT members, Canada maintained various policies and practices not wholly consistent with the letter and spirit of GATT.[30] Not only was the tariff

---

[27] The presence of high tariffs or escalating tariffs (tariffs that increase with the level of processing) leads to trade that takes advantage of holes or valleys in the tariff structure (zero or low rates of duty) while little or no trade takes place in items attracting higher rates. This can be illustrated by the fact that in 1945, before the GATT negotiations, US rates averaged around 30 percent but 67 percent of US imports entered duty free. In 1984, when US tariff levels averaged 5 percent, only 32 percent of US imports entered duty free. More goods were able to jump over the much lower rates. They could now compete, even when paying low rates. In fact, by the middle of the 1980s only about 70 percent of Canadian exports to the United States and about 70 percent of Canadian imports from the United States entered duty free; the frequently cited 80 percent figure was part of the press hype used to market the Tokyo Round results and reflected the trading patterns of 1976.

[28] The 1965 Canada-United States Automotive Products Trade Agreement provides for duty-free trade in specified automotive products. In the case of the United States, all imports that contain at least fifty percent combined Canadian and US content may be imported free of duty from Canada while in the case of Canada, qualified manufacturers may import the same automotive products duty-free from anywhere in the world as long as they meet certain performance requirements. The United States received a waiver from its MFN obligations to implement the agreement while Canada considered that it did not require a waiver, a decision that has never been challenged. See Carl Beigie, *The Canada-U.S. Automotive Agreement: An Evaluation* (Montreal: Canadian-American Committee, 1970). The long list of companies that attained Autopact status over the past twenty-five years is appended to chapter ten of the Free-Trade Agreement.

[29] The most detailed and up-to-date study of the Canadian economy can be found in the three-volume *Final Report* of the Royal Commission on the Economic Union and Development Prospects for Canada (Ottawa: Supply and Services, 1985) and its 71 volumes of supporting research (Toronto: University of Toronto Press, 1985).

[30] For a description of Canadian import and industrial policies see the federal government 1983 discussion paper, *A Review of Canadian Trade Policy* (Ottawa: Supply and Services, 1983); Peter Morici, Arthur J. R. Smith and Sperry Lea, *Canadian Industrial Policy* (Washington: National Planning Association, 1982); M. M. Hart, *Canadian Economic Development and the International*

high, but until recently Canada used unique valuation and classification systems which were out of step with the rest of the world; they were potent non-tariff barriers in their own right. Canada reluctantly agreed to change its valuation system in 1984 and introduced a modern classification system in 1988, thus quietly removing some of the lesser known trade restrictive elements of the National Policy. Canada also had a predilection for using duty remission programs, some of them frankly at odds with its international obligations. The Machinery Program was long a major thorn in the side of Canada's trading partners. Canadian provinces strengthened discriminatory wine and beer distribution systems to protect vintners and brewers, despite promises to do the opposite.[31] Even with the Autopact in place, Canada maintained an embargo against imports of used automobiles. It continued to apply discriminatory fish landing requirements. Discriminatory government procurement contracts were encrusted with offsets and other performance requirements. Until 1984, the Foreign Investment Review Agency maintained GATT-illegal export and domestic content requirements. In the 1950s Canadian negotiators pioneered the use of voluntary export restraints and orderly marketing arrangements, first with the Japanese and then with other Asian suppliers, to reduce competition in standard-technology products that proved able to surmount even the high levels of Canadian tariff protection. Finally, federal and provincial governments shielded producers of chickens, turkeys, eggs, milk, cheese, wheat, oats and barley from international competition through supply management and marketing schemes that require stiff import quotas.

To consolidate the mercantilist base of its domestic policies and to keep up with its major trading partners, Canada adopted a full-fledged contingency protection system in the *Special Import Measures Act* of 1984. Canadians frequently charge that the US system is protectionist – and it is – but the reality is that Canada has adopted an equally protectionist system of its own – as envisaged and provided for in GATT. Writes Peter Clark, an experienced Canadian trade practitioner, "The rules about dumping and subsidization are so detailed and complex that most companies are not aware they are (or may be) dumping or have accepted countervailable subsidies until they receive a notice of investi-

---

Trading System (Toronto: University of Toronto Press, 1985); Robert K. Paterson, *Canadian Regulation of International Trade and Investment* (Toronto: Carswell, 1986); and GATT, *Trade Policy Review 1990: Canada* (Geneva: GATT, forthcoming).

31   In 1979, as part of the Tokyo Round settlement, the Canadian provinces provided a letter of intent indicating that they would freeze existing practices and gradually phase out discriminatory pricing and listing practices over the next eight years. Their failure to translate intent into action, particularly on the part of Ontario, made the issue a key element in the FTA negotiations and led the EC to launch a GATT complaint. As a result, the provinces have now entered into more credible commitments to phase out their discriminatory practices.

gation."[32] The Tokyo Round Codes encouraged Canada and other smaller nations to adopt these schemes not because they were necessarily in their interest, but because they wanted to ensure that they could take full advantage of their GATT rights.

The GATT system allowed Canada to pursue a liberal-oriented foreign trade policy in Geneva while maintaining a much less liberal mix of domestic policies. At the same time, the policy mix enjoyed wide support and, until the advent of the debate about free trade with the United States, effectively removed trade policy from the front burner of public policy. The issues were ones that preoccupied professionals. The decisions required knowledge of details rather than of broad policy orientation. Ministers set the broad direction but were increasingly mystified by the esoterica of the detail. Because the basic policy orientation enjoyed broad support in the business sector, there was little cause for concern.

The ideological justification for all this was that as a small country dependent on trade with larger countries, Canada was in an unequal position and needed to take steps to defend its interests and boost its comparative advantage – a kind of infant industry argument applied to the country as a whole. The argument had strong emotional appeal but little intellectual foundation – it in effect denied the basic underpinnings of the open multilateral trading system which Canadian officials were trained to espouse in Geneva at the same time that they sought to circumvent it at home. The FTA provided an intellectually respectable basis for undoing this mindset. It is no wonder that some of the strongest initial opposition to the idea of a free-trade agreement with the United States came from officials deeply imbued with multilateral principles and steeped in Canada's earlier GATT experience.[33]

The Canada-US free-trade agreement marks a fundamental change in direction for Canada. It achieved three fundamental and reinforcing objectives:

- the most important, if least publicized, was to effect <u>domestic economic reform</u> by eliminating, at least for trade with the United States, the last vestiges of the National Policy and to constrain the more subtle new instruments of protection. More open borders would expose Canadian firms to

---

32 Peter Clark, "'Come into My Parlour': The United States and 'Unfair Trade'", Background Notes for a Presentation to the Institute for Political Involvement, December 3, 1984, p. 2.

33 The debate among officials prior to the government's decision to proceed with negotiations is told in Michael Hart, Bill Dymond and Colin Robertson, *Reconcilable Differences: The Rise and Triumph of Free Trade*, the manuscript of which is awaiting government clearance before publication.

greater international competition and encourage them to restructure and modernize and become more efficient and productive.

- the most publicized was to provide a <u>bulwark against US protectionism</u>. By gaining more secure and open access to the large, contiguous US market, Canadian business would be able to plan and grow with greater confidence and gain an incentive to accept the challenge of increased competition from the United States.

- finally, the agreement was meant to provide an improved and more <u>modern basis for managing the Canada-US relationship</u>. Since 1948, the GATT had served this function but had increasingly proved inadequate. New and more enforceable rules combined with more sophisticated institutional machinery would put the relationship on a more predictable and less confrontational footing.[34]

Achieving these goals required a wrenching debate in Canada and a fundamental re-ordering of priorities. The debate reflected two visions of Canada and of the role of government in society – the one characterized by economic nationalism and an emphasis on the need for an active interventionist government to direct economic life, the other by economic internationalism and a reliance on market forces to order economic life. The first wanted to isolate Canada from the world and feared the wider implications of economic interdependence and integration; the second wanted Canada to take an active role in the world and was confident Canadian values and priorities would survive closer economic integration. The actual negotiations and the resulting agreement sometimes seemed only incidental to the debate. It was a debate about fundamental values and perceptions.[35]

---

[34] In addition to the writings of private sector analysts and advocates of freer trade with the United States, the government's 1982-83 trade policy review and the final report of the Macdonald Royal Commission were particularly important in shaping Canadian objectives. See Department of External Affairs, *A Review of Canadian Trade Policy* (Ottawa: Supply and Services, 1983) and Royal Commission on the Economic Union and Development Prospects for Canada, *Report* (Ottawa: Supply and Services, 1985). A handy overview of official attitudes at the beginning of the negotiations is provided by Department of External Affairs, *Canadian Trade Negotiations: Introduction, Selected Documents, Further Reading* (Ottawa: Supply and Services, 1986).

[35] In many ways the debate marked the culmination of twenty-five years of intellectual ferment reflected in the competing views of the Economic Council of Canada and the Science Council of Canada. Founded in the 1960s, the two councils adopted diametrically opposed views of the best policy mix for Canada. The Economic Council, in its reports and supporting research volumes, consistently advocated open markets and greater integration into the global economy, the best remembered statement being its 1975 report *Looking Outward: A New Trade*

The FTA institutionalizes the internationalist view of Canada and catches up to the economic and business realities of the Canada-US trade and investment relationship. By guaranteeing more open and more secure access to businesses on both sides of the border, it allows both countries to plan and grow with increased confidence. Early evidence that the FTA is meeting this economic objective can be seen in the changed attitudes among Canadian entrepreneurs. Canada may be dependent on exports for 30 per cent of its GNP, but traditionally exports have been confined to a narrow range of products. Additionally, few Canadian companies were involved in international business. Many sectors of the Canadian economy did not view their business as international or take the steps necessary to become successful on a worldwide basis. Over the past few years, however, the business pages of Canada's newspapers have shown a remarkable change in these attitudes, changes directly attributable to the debate over the Canada-US negotiations and their positive result. An increasing number of Canadian companies, including those already involved in exporting, now acknowledge the need to become more internationally competitive, to rationalize their production and to produce products for the world market rather than only for the Canadian or North American markets. They have accepted the challenge to diversify, establish joint ventures, enter into licensing arrangements and distribution networks and establish branch plants or subsidiaries to an unprecedented extent. They now view the US market as not only vital in itself but also as an intermediate step to the world market.

The Agreement is underwriting rationalization and specialization which in turn should lead to an increase in intra-industry trade and even intra-firm trade. The success of these efforts will be evident if Canadian trading patterns diversify – not as a result of a reduction in trade with the United States but because of an increase in trade across the Atlantic and Pacific due to greater competitiveness and specialization. The ultimate economic success of the Agreement, therefore, will require the successful implementation of outward-looking, international business attitudes. The dynamism resulting from these changed attitudes will lead to much more wealth creation than the mere removal of tariffs. The long-term success of the agreement will depend critically on this type of dynamic economic adjustment.

The United States: Return to the Protectionist Womb

While the FTA confirmed a more market-oriented trade policy in Canada, it arrested the drift toward more protection in the United States, at least insofar as

---

Strategy for Canada. The Science Council, on the other hand, consistently advocated the need for an active, interventionist industrial policy, including more import barriers if needed, best expressed in *Forging the Links: A Technology Policy for Canada* (1979).

trade with Canada is concerned. In the immediate post-war years, American officials took pride in the assertion that the United States was the most open market in the world. One Administration after another took steps to make the world trading system increasingly more open. The rhetoric has remained, even though the reality has changed. The United States has tilted back to its historic protectionist stance.[36]

Protectionism has deep and enduring roots in the United States. From the Continental Congress to the Smoot-Hawley tariff of 1930, US legislators shielded US producers from world competition.[37] The cost of this protectionism was easily borne by an expanding continental economy. For a brief period, from the *Reciprocal Trade Agreements Act* of 1934 until the Nixon economic measures of 1971 (ushering in a surtax and devaluing the US dollar), the US adopted a liberal, outward-looking trade policy to advance its broad, world-wide economic and political interests. The combined effect of the excesses of the depression and of US economic and political hegemony had convinced a skeptical Congress to accept this direction. Congress, less out of conviction favouring multilateral freer trade and more in an effort to shield itself from the pleading of special interests, was prepared to adopt four complementary techniques that allowed the Administration to chart a new direction for US trade policy:

- delegation of first its tariff and later of its non-tariff negotiating authority to the President, giving the Administration the capacity to negotiate reciprocal tariff-reducing and rule-making agreements;
- development of a quasi-judicial trade remedy system that allowed US industries to seek relief from injurious imports through administrative tribunals rather than as a result of industry-specific legislation;
- occasional special deals for politically potent sectors such as agriculture, textiles and clothing and steel that stood outside the international and national rules but allowed those rules to continue to operate for the rest of the economy; and
- creation of a special office in the White House, the Special Trade Representative (now United States Trade Representative) to act as a broker among

---

[36] The latest detailed description of US trade law and policy can be found in GATT, *Trade Policy Review 1989: The United States of America* (Geneva: GATT, 1990). Sidney Weintraub in chapter 4 of *A Marriage of Convenience: Relations Between Mexico and the United States* (New York: Oxford University Press, 1990) describes the impact of the return to protectionism in the United States on Mexico.

[37] The intellectual roots of US protectionism go back to Alexander Hamilton's *Report on the Subject of Manufactures* to the US House of Representatives in 1791. See Robert Gilpin, *The Political Economy of International Relations* (Princeton: Princeton University Press, 1987), pp. 180-181.

competing interests at arm's length from the Congress and equipped with some of the political clout of the presidency.

These four techniques allowed the congressional leadership to acquiesce in relatively liberal trade policies without having to accept political responsibility for them. It also allowed the Administration to pursue complementary trade and foreign policies. The whole system was run by technocrats and effectively removed trade policy from the agenda of high policy.[38]

But by the 1970s the conditions that had allowed a liberal trade policy had lost force and relevance and US trade policy began to revert to its fundamental protectionist habits. Major sectors such as autos, consumer electronics, textiles and steel wilted before significant import penetration. Burgeoning trade deficits and the re-emergence of Europe and Japan as major industrial powers deprived the United States of unquestioned trade and economic dominance and revived the mercantilist proposition that imports constitute strategic weakness and exports represent strength. Notes the Bilateral Commission on the Future of United States-Mexico Relations:

> Rapid increases in import penetration, unsustainable high levels of imports, and adjustment problems in key sectors (like automobiles and agriculture) have made many U.S. politicians, government bureaucrats, and businessmen more receptive to managed trade. This has raised questions about the depth of the U.S. commitment to open markets that sustained the postwar trading system.[39]

The traditional private sector supporters of a liberal trade policy, such as export-oriented resource and grains producers and competitive capital intensive manu-

---

[38] Some analysts believe that the demise of US commitment to liberalism can in part be explained by the fact that its commitment was driven more by strategic than economic considerations and that it is the strategic considerations that have been overwhelmed by protectionist interests. In *Protectionism* (Cambridge, Mass: MIT Press, 1988), Jagdish Bhagwati reviews the various theses developed by US analysts to explain both American post-war liberalism and the more recent retreat.

[39] Bilateral Commission on the Future of United States-Mexico Relations, *The Challenge of Interdependence: Mexico and the United States* (New York: University Press of America, 1989), p. 63. In a similar vein, Bill Brock and Bob Hormats write: "For those of us in the United States, the glory days of unchallenged economic superiority have been replaced by years of monumental economic challenges on our own turf by Japan, the increasingly dynamic economies of Asia (the new tigers), as well as the resurgent nations of Europe. ... There is a dangerous tendency to believe that our economy is so inherently strong that it will thrive no matter what policies are applied to it, and a similar dangerous tendency to blame many of our problems on the trade practices or competitive strategy of other nations." William E. Brock and Robert D Hormats, eds., *The Global Economy: America's Role in the Decade Ahead* (New York: W. W. Norton, 1990), pp. 7-8.

facturers, found their ability to compete both at home and abroad less sure than a generation earlier. There were now many more competitors; the subsidy practices of the Europeans and developing countries undercut US producers; and, in the early 1980s, the high value of the dollar further undermined their position on world markets.

The decline in support for a liberal trade policy was paralleled by the steadily growing exposure of the US economy to world trade. In 1950, exports constituted only six percent of US GNP. By the 1980s, that figure was approaching ten percent. At the same time, the US began to experience an almost continuous deficit in its merchandise trade surplus; since 1970, the US has run a merchandise trade deficit in every year but two. The ratio of combined exports and imports to GDP rose from 8.8 percent in 1972 to 22 percent in 1987, largely fuelled by the growth in imports, particularly manufactured imports.[40] Throughout the Reagan years, the United States ran not only a merchandise trade deficit but also a current account deficit as rising imports of consumer goods far outstripped service receipts and, by the middle of the decade, a devalued US dollar fuelled by US budgetary deficits began to suck in foreign capital. By 1988, US indebtedness to the rest of the world had reached half a trillion dollars.[41]

Congress thus found an increasing number of dissatisfied industrial groups on its doorstep, complaining that the Administration was insensitive to their concerns and the trade remedy laws inadequate to their needs. In response, Congress began steadily to reassert its constitutional authority over US trade policy.[42] Rather than reverting to the ancient technique of the tariff and quotas, Congress now used four new techniques to goad the Administration into a more accommodating (i.e., less liberal) approach to trade policy:

- omnibus legislation facilitating access by private interests to US trade remedy law. The *Trade Expansion Act* of 1962, setting out authority for the Kennedy Round, was the last act under the old regime. The 1974 *Trade Act*

---

[40] Bilateral Commission on the Future of United States-Mexico Relations, *The Challenge of Interdependence: Mexico and the United States* (New York: University Press of America, 1989), p. 59.

[41] Bilateral Commission on the Future of United States-Mexico Relations, *The Challenge of Interdependence: Mexico and the United States* (New York: University Press of America, 1989), p. 46.

[42] For an analysis of the return of US congressional protectionism, see I. M. Destler, *American Trade Politics: System Under Stress* (Washington: Institute for International Economics, 1986). An abbreviated version can be found in "Protecting Congress or Protecting Trade?" *Foreign Policy*, vol. 62 (Spring, 1986), pp. 96-107. For a fascinating comparison of late nineteenth century British arguments against unilateral free trade and those of US proponents of reciprocity, see Jagdish N. Bhagwati and Douglas A. Irwin, "The Return of the Reciprocitarians," *The World Economy*, 1986, pp. 109-130.

Chart 2
Principal US Trade-Remedy Laws

Statute	Focus	Criteria	Available Remedies	Administrative Authorities
Sec. 201 ("escape clause")	injurious imports	increasing imports are a substantial cause of serious injury	duties; quotas; tariff-rate quotas; adjustment assistance; orderly marketing arrangements	USITC President[a]
Sec. 701	subsidized imports	material injury [b]	countervailing duties	USITC ITA
Sec. 731	dumping (selling at less than fair value)	material injury	antidumping duties	USITC ITA
Sec. 301	violations of trade agreements & commitments	actions are unreasonable, unjustified or discriminatory	"all appropriate and feasible action"	USTR President
Sec. 337	unfair trade practices (for example, trademark or patent infringement)	actions destroy or substantially injure an industry.	exclusion orders; cease and desist orders	USITC President
Sec. 338	foreign country discrimination	burden or disadvantage US commerce	increase duties, exclusion	President
Sec. 22	agricultural imports below US prices	material interference with price support programs	import fees quotas	USITC USDA President
Sec. 406	disruptive imports from communist countries	significant cause of material injury	duties quotas	USITC President
Sec. 332	any trade irritant	effect on US industry	investigation	USITC
Sec. 232	increasing imports	threat to national security	investigation range of restrictive measures	Commerce President
ITA: International Trade Administration of the US Department of Commerce				
USDA: US Department of Agriculture				
USTR: Office of the US Trade Representative				
USITC: US International Trade Commission				
a. The Congress may override the President.				
b. The material injury test is only extended to countries that fulfill certain conditions.				

ushered in the new regime, with Congress trading authority for the Tokyo Round for revisions in trade remedy legislation. Subsequent acts further revised the laws to broaden their scope and coverage and reduce administrative discretion so that US industries would be more likely to qualify for import relief. The 1988 *Trade and Competitiveness Act* represented the latest unilateral redefinition of existing trade rules, although the final version did not include some of the more egregious efforts of earlier drafts to rewrite US international trade obligations.

- product-specific legislation imposing new barriers to imports. From the *Agriculture Adjustment Act* of 1933 through the *Trade and Competitiveness Act* of 1988, Congress has been prepared to legislate protection for favoured sectors, even where such protection has run counter to US international obligations. In the mid-1950s, the US needed a waiver from its GATT obligations to accommodate agricultural protectionism and has steadily sought new derogations from international rules to satisfy the political clout of the textile industry. More recently, congressional pressure has convinced the Administration to pursue voluntary export restraints on shoes, automobiles, steel and semi-conductors; the Administration has convinced itself that without such GATT-illegal measures, worse restrictions on imports would be legislated.

- encouraging more aggressive use of existing legislation and administrative discretion. The introduction of section 301 in the *Trade Act* of 1974[43] gave US producers a potent weapon to force the Administration to pursue their complaints; that provision was strengthened in 1988. One of its favourite techniques is the voluntary import obligation which, for example, has forced Japan to open its semi-conductor, tobacco and leather markets to American producers on a bilateral rather than on an MFN basis. Since 1980, the number of countervailing, antidumping, unfair trade (section 337) and safeguard cases has steadily mounted, now averaging over 200 a year, as the Administration, under congressional pressure, has methodically lowered its standard for acceptance of petitions. The scope of cases has been resolutely expanded to cover insignificant volumes of trade with devastating psychological effect – if small amounts of trade can be caught in the web, what could happen to significant trade volumes?[44]

---

43 This section authorizes the President to take action to enforce US trade agreement rights against foreign government policies that are "unjustifiable, unreasonable and discriminatory" and that burden or restrict US international commerce. Over the years, Congress has tightened its provisions, reducing administrative discretion and forcing the President to act against "unfair" trading practices.

44 For example, in the Oil Country Tubular Goods case involving both dumping and subsidization, the Canadian share of the US import market was less than 6.5%. In the Cut Flowers case, also alleging both dumping and subsidization, the issue was carried to ridiculous extremes: Canadian exports represented some $200,000 out of total world imports of only $17 million. In Egg Filler Flats (dumping) and Probe Thermostats (subsidization), small Canadian companies were harassed by their US competitors in unsuccessful efforts to keep them out of the market, at great and fruitless expense to all concerned.

- increasing restrictions on government procurement. Congress has steadily increased the ambit and depth of Buy America procurement preferences by adding riders to defence appropriations and federal funding programs, thus effectively shielding a huge volume of US production from foreign competition.

The favourite justification for these departures from the letter and spirit of GATT used by US policy-makers is two-fold and interrelated: the first is the deeply held conviction that the US market is the most open in the world and only the US plays by the rules – other countries openly flout the rules and are taking advantage of US generosity. All that the US is trying to do is to "level the playing field." Thus any US departures are but minor imperfections in a world of much greater sinners. The second argument is that "small" doses of protectionism are required to satisfy the real protectionists and prevent much worse – the fair trade laws and the escape clauses are thus portrayed as a kind of inoculation against a full-scale outbreak of protectionism. Like the Canadian arguments, they have little intellectual foundation but a lot of political appeal.[45]

In order further to salve their consciences, US officials often sponsor multilateral negotiations to rewrite the rules and thus provide international cover for US practice.[46] The 1955 GATT waiver allowing the US to impose restrictions on agricultural imports in the absence of domestic production restraint programs (which would have brought them into conformity with article XI), effectively removed agriculture from the GATT rules. The 1961 Short-term Cotton Textiles Arrangement (followed by a long-term arrangement and four manifestations of a multifibre arrangement) removed textiles and clothing, but only for low-cost producers (read LDC and state-trading countries), from the general rules. The Kennedy and Tokyo Round antidumping and antisubsidy codes provided international cover for the highly discriminatory contingency protection system now in full flower.[47] These initiatives, often opposed by the European Community until such

---

45 See Robert S. Spich, "Free Trade as Ideology, Fair Trade as Goal: Problems of an Ideological Approach to U.S. Trade Policy," *International Trade Journal* vol. 1, no. 2 (Winter, 1986), pp. 129-154 and Raymond Vernon, "International Trade Policy in the 1980s: Prospects and Problems," *International Studies Quarterly,* vol. 26, no. 4 (December 1982), pp. 483-510.

46 This mental habit is evident throughout the US submission to the GATT justifying its trade policies. The text is reproduced in GATT, *Trade Policy Review 1989: The United States of America* (Geneva: GATT, 1990).

47 Commenting on Canadian draft legislation to implement the Tokyo Round Agreements, Rodney Grey wrote: "The key factor now at work is the impact of U.S. concepts on the drafting of international agreements. In implementing Canadian Tokyo Round obligations, and in rewriting Canadian law to take advantage of GATT and Tokyo Round agreement rights, Canadian draftsmen are translating into Canadian legal phraseology the words and phrases

time as parallel action was taken in Europe, have gradually shifted the primary focus of GATT negotiations from trade liberalization to trade management and added to cynicism about the value of an open multilateral trading system.

As the United States enters the 1990s, three forces contend for the direction of American trade policy. One represents the traditional multilateral orthodoxy which fuelled US leadership in the erection and maintenance of the multilateral trading system and drives the US position in the Uruguay Round. The second is a resurgence of unilateralism and protectionism in US trade policy, disdainful and distrustful of the multilateral trading system. The third favours the negotiation of regional or bilateral agreements with selected countries notably Canada, Mexico and those of the Pacific Rim, either on their own merits or as a complement to the Uruguay Round of multilateral trade negotiations.[48]

It is, of course, possible for a superpower like the United States to ride off in several directions at once for a considerable period of time. In the practice of trade policy, consistency is a virtue much honoured in the breach by both great and small powers. Indeed, both current US trade policy and the debate about its direction in the Administration, the Congress and the US business community blur the distinctions.

Nevertheless, the multilateralist position has lost some of its potency; it is no longer the preeminent and unchallenged position; the geopolitical impulses that, until recently, successfully subordinated trade policy to US foreign policy, have lost their authority.[49] The unilateralists, while paying lip service to the multilateral ideal, appeal to deeply-embedded US mercantilism and strike an emotionally powerful chord in the American psyche. For their part, the regionalists and bilateralists are struggling to find a patch of secure ground by marrying the liberal virtues of the traditional multilateral approach to a recognition that the future may lie in tailor-made trade agreements with particular countries and regions.

---

of the agreements that so frequently are American words and phrases." *U.S. Trade Policy Legislation* (Montreal: Institute for Research on Public Policy, 1982), p. 95.

[48] A more detailed examination of the various strains in American trade policy, including the new fascination with bilateralism, can be found in William A. Dymond, "Lord Ronald and United States Trade Policy," in Michael Hart, ed., *Essays in Canadian Trade Policy* (Ottawa: Centre for Trade Policy and Law, forthcoming). I am grateful to Mr. Dymond for allowing me to use parts of that paper in this study.

[49] For a clear statement of multilateral orthodoxy, see Michael Aho and Jonathan Aronson, *Trade Talks: America Had Better Listen!* (New York: Council on Foreign Relations, 1986).

The 1987 FTA institutionalizes the liberal, outward-looking trade policy that reigned in the United States until the early 1970s. Whether US protectionism flourishes or fades in the future, the agreement restores security and predictability of Canadian access to the US market. The overall effect of the agreement is to create a privileged trade relationship between Canada and the United States and to constitute a continuing agenda and permanent mechanism to address current and future trade and investment issues. As such it provides a prudent backstop to the GATT system by creating a formidable institutional and statutory shield against either legislated or administrative US protectionism. Finally, it enhances bilateral control over the trading rules between Canada and the United States. Under the MFN rule, reductions in trade barriers between the two countries inevitably raised questions of extending unrequited benefits to third countries, always a politically difficult if economically rational proposition. For the United States, until the conclusion of the FTA, this had always proved a significant obstacle to reducing barriers to Canadian exports except in the framework of multilateral trade negotiations.

Mexico and the US Bilateralists

Mexican interest in a bilateral accord with the United States has been strengthened by an astute reading of the ascendancy of the bilateralists among US decision-makers. The notion that bilateral or regional agreements provide a viable option for US trade policy is, of course, not new. The trade agreements which flowed from the 1934 *Reciprocal Trade Agreements Act* were all bilateral arrangements, including the 1935 and 1938 agreements with Canada and the 1942 agreement with Mexico. The 1979 *Trade Agreements Act* called for a study of trade agreements with countries of the northern portion of the western hemisphere. The 1984 *Trade and Tariffs Act* provided for the negotiation of bilateral agreements with Israel and any other country which so requested the negotiation of a bilateral agreement. In 1985, a bilateral US-Israel agreement came into effect followed by the Canada-US Free Trade Agreement of 1987. Mexico has now emerged as the most viable candidate for the next agreement with the United States. Even committed multilateralists are prepared to concede that the agreement with Canada and a possible agreement with Mexico are acceptable.[50]

There is considerable irony in the US focus on Mexico, given that the interest in the bilateral or regional option arises from the frustration of the United States with the GATT. As noted above, Mexico only became a contracting party to the

---

[50] See C. Michael Aho in "More Bilateral Trade Agreements Would be a Blunder: What the New President Should Do," *Cornell International Law Journal*, vol. 22, no. 1 (Winter, 1989), pp. 25-38 and Jeffrey Schott, "More Free Trade Areas?" in his *Free Trade Areas and U.S. Trade Policy* (Washington: Institute for International Economics, 1988).

GATT in 1986 and under the Salinas Administration has embarked upon an ambitious set of policies designed to liberalize the economy and integrate it into the multilateral trading framework embodied by the GATT. At the same time, the US interest in a bilateral approach to Mexico springs from a desire to support and encourage these policies combined with a sense of duty arising from the intimate (if not always happy) relationship between the two countries.

It is these geopolitical considerations that are overcoming the traditional reluctance of US multilateralists and protectionists to reach a bilateral accommodation with Mexico. They accept that for the first time since the 1940s there may be an opportunity to negotiate an accord that would commit the Mexican economy willingly and firmly to the market system. It is an opportunity that may not be repeated in the foreseeable future if the US fails to respond. A US-Mexico accord would underwrite American investment in Mexico and strengthen the hand of those in Mexico who favour American-style democracy. An economically healthy Mexico would stand as a strong object lesson to the troubled countries of Central and South America and give the United States a staunch ally in regaining the trust of these countries. They see a bilateral trade and investment agreement as the most acceptable way to deal with illegal Mexican immigration and to tackle the illicit drug trade. A vibrant and growing Mexican economy would be able to absorb a much larger share of its growing labour force and provide alternatives to drug trafficking, thus reducing the pressure on the US border of both drugs and migrant workers. Finally, President Bush and some of his advisors see the Canada-US agreement and a possible US-Mexico agreement as stepping stones to greater economic cooperation involving all of the Western Hemisphere.

While these geopolitical considerations may be of greatest moment to the United States, they are not unimportant to Canadians. Canada shares with the United States an interest in fostering the development of a strong, market-oriented democracy in Latin America. Its decision to join the Organization of American States (OAS) last year underscores this point. The prospects for lasting peace and stability in Central America, for example, would be considerably enhanced by greater hemispheric economic cooperation. Resolving the problems of the drug trade would also be advanced by an agreement. Canada, too, would gain in stature in Latin America by participating in a tripartite arrangement. These factors perhaps contributed to Prime Minister Mulroney's enthusiastic statements during his visit to Mexico in March, 1990. He is quoted as saying:

> This hemisphere is going to emerge as an economic giant. Brazil, Mexico, Venezuela ...
> these are going to be economic giants of the next century, so it will be to the advantage of
> the U.S. and Canada to begin building bridges, building trading instruments with them. I

think the fact that Canada initiated discussions on free trade with the United States indicates that Canada doesn't intend to be left out of anything.[51]

While a US-Mexico agreement would undoubtedly fortify the development of a
market-oriented Mexican economy, Canadian participation is likely to have a further beneficial political impact by reducing nationalist sensitivities.

Much as with Canada, the United States left the initiative to Mexico, given the
danger that a US move could arouse Mexican nationalism. While the nature of
any bilateral agreement between the mature US economy and the developing
Mexican economy is not yet clear, there is now broad acceptance in Washington
that the overall US-Mexican relationship will require a substantive bilateral trade
agreement in the relatively near future. As a result, the Mexicans, for their part,
are actively considering to what extent a Canada-US-style FTA is negotiable,
having concluded that more limited approaches aimed at specific tariffs and sectors are insufficient. The June 11 Bush-Salinas communiqué now commits the
two governments to the negotiation of a bilateral agreement.

Mexican interest in negotiating with the United States has been made more
urgent by its anxiety that US attention may increasingly be diverted across the
Pacific and Atlantic. Mexicans witnessed in the 1980s the effect of excessive US
preoccupation with Japan, and they fear that remaining energy may soon be concentrated on the rapidly evolving situation in Europe, and particularly Eastern
Europe. They do not want Mexico to be sidelined just as it emerges from its protectionist cocoon.

Additionally, Mexican leaders see the unified marketplace of the EC and potential market rationalization in Eastern Europe as strong competition for
European, Japanese and American investment capital. Salinas concluded that
"the changes in Eastern Europe showed me that [world] competition for resources and markets will strengthen."[52] His January 1990 visit to Europe also
drove home that European investors were not looking much beyond Eastern
Europe. At the same time, Salinas astutely observed that developments in
Eastern Europe would provide EC companies with a source of low-cost labour to
help make European products more competitive on world markets. EC industrialists are moving quickly to make this a reality. Salinas reasons that the right
kind of North American arrangement could do the same for North American industries. Failure to encourage this kind of creative and dynamic adjustment will
allow industries across the Atlantic and Pacific to forge too far ahead of those in

---

51   Quoted in *The Ottawa Citizen,* March 18, 1990 and *The Globe & Mail,* March 19, 1990.
52   Quoted in Bruce Stokes, "Trade Talks with Mexico Face Hurdles," *National Journal,* June 16,
     1990, p. 1486.

North America. Salinas told reporters in Washington that Mexico wants to export goods rather than people. "To us, free trade means more job creation and less immigration to the United States."[53]

The combined weight of these events and developments has made the <u>idea</u> of a North American free-trade area an attractive policy choice in all three countries. The time has come, therefore, to take the issue a step further and look at it from a more narrow trade and commercial perspective. While broad geopolitical and institutional developments may provide an atmosphere within which the desire to negotiate takes on new urgency, the success of any trade negotiation will depend on whether there is sufficient commonality of interest on trade and economic grounds.

🍎🍎🍎🍎🍎

---

[53] Quoted in *The New York Times,* June 11, 1990.

4

North American
Trade and Investment Patterns

Just as the policy framework for trade and investment evolved over the 1980s, the patterns of trade and investment also changed. The relatively unsophisticated nature of US-Mexico trade and the almost complete absence of Canada-Mexico trade in the 1960s and 1970s have gradually given way to growing de facto integration. The situation as it existed a decade ago gave a practical foundation to the lack of interest in a North American free-trade agreement. Circumstances today underline why there is increasing interest in the negotiation of such an agreement, particularly in the United States and Mexico, but also in Canada.

US-Mexico Trade Relations

Mexico is currently the United States' fourth largest trading partner, after Canada, Japan and the EC, accounting for approximately 6-7 percent of US exports and imports (see table 6). The United States, on the other hand, is Mexico's dominant trading partner, responsible for two-thirds of both exports and imports and far outdistancing Mexican trade with Europe, Japan, the rest of Latin America and Canada (see table 7).

Prior to the mid-1970s, Mexican exports were evenly balanced between manufactures and resources, primarily agricultural goods. From the mid-1970s until the mid-1980s, oil dominated Mexican exports. Since then, oil has gradually receded in importance to be replaced by manufactures (see chart 1). For the United States, manufactures have always dominated its exports to Mexico.

Table 6
Geographic Distribution of US Merchandise Trade
(percent)

Trading Partner	1985		1987	
	Exports	Imports	Exports	Imports
Canada	22.2	20.0	23.7	17.5
Mexico	6.4	5.5	5.8	5.0
EC	21.5	18.8	24.0	20.0
Japan	10.6	19.9	11.2	20.8
Other Latin America	6.7	7.0	6.7	5.9
Rest of World	32.7	28.8	28.7	30.7

Source: US Department of Commerce, *Statistical Abstract of the United States*, 1987 and 1989. Totals may not add due to rounding.

Oil was a major Mexican export in the early part of this century but with the nationalization of the oil companies in 1938, exports dried up, not to be revived until 1974. With the rapid rise in world prices and the discovery of major new reserves, the Mexican authorities agreed to enter into export contracts in the hope of using oil revenues to finance economic development. Exports took off rapidly reaching a peak of US$15.6 billion in 1982, representing 73.6 percent of total exports. With the fall in prices from 1982 on, however, oil receipts have steadily declined and accounted for only US$5.9 billion in 1988 or 28.4 percent of total exports.[1] With the disappearance of oil as a major earner of foreign exchange, Mexico has been forced to find markets for its manufactures and make them more competitive on world markets in order to service its huge foreign debt. The reform program outlined in chapter three has had some success, principally in exports to the United States, amounting to US$23.2 billion in 1988, of which only US$3.3 billion was in receipts for oil (see table 8).

Economic restructuring has made Mexico a lucrative market for US producers of capital equipment and other manufactures, which accounted for more than US$15.0 billion in sales in 1988. In return, Mexico has begun to penetrate the US market with a wider range of intermediate and final goods. Its share of the US market for traditional low-cost exports such as textiles, clothing and shoes has

---

[1] Nisso Bucay and Eduardo Perez Motta, "Mexico," chapter 6 in John Whalley, ed., *Dealing with the North: Developing Countries and the Global Trading System* (London: Centre for the Study of International Economic Relations, 1987), p. 212 and Banco Nacional de Mexico, *Basic Statistics*, (Mexico City, 1989).

remained low as a result of stiff US quotas. In their place, Mexico has been able to make inroads with more sophisticated products (See table 8 and chart 3).

Table 7
Geographic Distribution of Mexico's Merchandise Trade
(percent)

Trading Partner	1983		1985		1987	
	Exports	Imports	Exports	Imports	Exports	Imports
United States	58.2	63.8	61.2	67.9	64.7	64.6
EC[a]	10.2	13.9	10.3	13.2	14.6	16.2
Japan	6.9	4.4	7.9	5.6	6.5	6.5
Latin America	7.8	3.7	5.8	4.8	7.5	2.9
Canada	1.9	2.4	1.7	1.6	1.5	2.7
Others	15.0	12.2	14.2	7.0	5.1	7.0

a. includes Greece, Spain and Portugal for 1987 only.
Source: adapted from Sidney Weintraub, *Marriage of Convenience,* Tables 4.1 and 4.2.

Table 8
Mexican Merchandise Trade with the United States

	1987		1988	
	Exports	Imports	Exports	Imports
		(Thousands of US dollars)		
Food and live animals	2,072,492	670,137	1,927,264	1,517,245
Beverages and Tobacco	270,981	11,563	264,525	22,469
Crude materials, inedible, exc. fuel	276,165	1,049,957	368,846	1,464,790
Mineral fuels, lubrcnts, related matr.	3,856,901	510,256	3,314,478	458,034
Oils and fats, animal & vegetable	3,705	95,363	8,330	142,023
Chemicals and related products	507,055	1,450,862	724,466	1,833,657
Manufactured goods by chief material	2,006,895	1,541,672	2,466,126	2,262,185
Machinery and transport equipment	8,727,248	7,333,203	10,928,273	10,089,075
Miscellaneous mfrd. artcls, nspf	1,776,571	1,337,181	2,279,395	1,983,279
Articles not provided for elsewhere	772,773	569,361	995,187	860,505
Total	20,270,785	14,569,554	23,276,890	20,633,263

Note for tables 8, 9 and 11: The commodity groupings have been taken from the US Department of Commerce material listed below; in the case of the Canadian statistics (now based on the Harmonized System) these groupings do not necessarily coincide and their values may have been estimated. **Sources:** Statistics Canada, *Exports by Country: January-December 1989 (H.S. Based)* and *Imports by Country: January-December 1989 (H.S. Based)* (Ottawa: Minister of Supply and Services Canada, 1990). U.S. Department of Commerce, *U.S. Foreign Trade Highlights: 1988* (Washington D.C.: U.S. Department of Commerce, 1989). International Bank for Reconstruction and Development, *The World Bank Atlas 1989* (Washington D.C.: The World Bank, 1989). The figures include trade involving Maquiladora plants.

Until the 1980s, US-Mexico trade took place without the benefit of any formal trade agreement. The 1942 reciprocal trade agreement was allowed to lapse in 1950 and no replacement was negotiated.[2] As a result, any disputes were dealt with on an ad hoc basis and the United States and Mexico extended each other most-favoured-nation treatment without any contractual obligation. Given the relative importance of Mexican trade to the United States in the 1970s and 1980s, it is not surprising that the United States was one of the most supportive sponsors of Mexican accession to GATT in 1979. It played a prominent role in the Working Party on Mexican accession and reached a generous settlement with Mexico in a Tokyo Round tariff negotiation that anticipated Mexican accession. The decision by President Lopez Portillo not to proceed with Mexican membership, in part due to fear of increased US influence, was thus seen as a blow to US prestige and interests and complicated US-Mexico relations. To offset the potential for problems and urged on by the Mexico-U.S. Business Committee, Presidents Reagan and Portillo established a Joint Commission on Trade and Commerce in 1981, but it met with little success.[3]

Chart 3
Commodity Distribution of Mexican Exports
(1976, 1980, 1985, 1989)

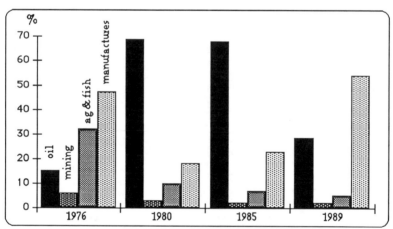

Source: Adapted from Sidney Weintraub, *Mexican Trade Policy and the North American Community,* p. 13.

---

2   Peter Murphy, "U.S.-Mexico Trade talks: A Preview of What's to Come," *Report on Free Trade,* April 23, 1990, p. 7.

3   Peter Murphy, "U.S.-Mexico Trade talks: A Preview of What's to Come," *Report on Free Trade,* April 23, 1990, p. 7.

The US initially considered the 1985 reform program and the 1986 renewed request for GATT membership with some caution but nevertheless reacted positively to Mexican overtures to improve the basis for trade. In 1985, the United States signed its first trade agreement with Mexico in more than a generation, agreeing to extend to Mexico the benefits of the injury test under its countervail procedures in return for Mexican discipline on export subsidies. At the same time, the two governments issued a statement of intent to negotiate a broader framework agreement. The United States again played a prominent role in the GATT accession Working Party and welcomed Mexican accession in 1986, although this time on terms less generous than seven years earlier. There was no anticipatory tariff deal as there had been in 1979.[4]

The following year, the United States and Mexico concluded a framework agreement providing for enhanced consultations and streamlined dispute settlement procedures.[5] The negotiation of this agreement as well as discussions under it, built confidence in the capacity of the two parties to negotiate and led in 1989 to a more substantive understanding. Notes Peter Murphy, chief American negotiator of the 1987 agreement:

> The agreement has provided a key management tool by offering a non-political forum for improving understanding of respective trade and investment policies, correcting misunderstandings, influencing the development of Mexican sectoral development programs, seeking changes in investment policies, improving market access, and providing a mechanism for addressing specific problems.[6]

The October 1989 Understanding signed by Presidents Bush and Salinas in Washington called for much more intensive work by the two sides in identifying sectors and issues for negotiation in addition to maintaining a framework for consultation and dispute settlement. In parallel with work pursued under the Understanding, the two governments have since agreed on specific commitments on steel, textiles and clothing (Mexico will continue to restrain its exports but at higher levels) and on intellectual property and standards (Mexico will provide

---

4 Sidney Weintraub, *Mexican Trade Policy and the North American Community* (Washington: Center for Strategic and International Studies, 1988) and Nisso Bucay and Eduardo Perez Motta, "Trade Negotiation Strategy for Mexico," in John Whalley, ed., *The Small Among the Big* (London: Centre for the Study of International Economic Relations, 1988).

5 See Guy C. Smith, "The United States-Mexico Framework Agreement: Implementation for Bilateral Trade," *Law and Policy in International Business,* vol. 20, no. 4 (1989), pp. 655-681.

6 Peter Murphy, "U.S.-Mexico Trade Talks: A Preview of What's to Come," *Report on Free Trade,* April 23, 1990, p. 7.

higher levels of protection and move to harmonize its standards with those of the United States).[7]

Despite the lack of formal intergovernmental agreement between the two countries until the last few years, two unilateral US trade programs influenced the development of US-Mexico trade. The introduction by the United States of its generalized system of preferences (GSP) in 1976 proved to be of substantial benefit to Mexico, and Mexican exports rapidly took advantage of the improved access, becoming one of the major beneficiaries of the program after Taiwan, Korea and Brazil.[8] Less than 10 percent of Mexico's exports to the United States, however, benefit from the GSP program.[9]

Of much greater importance was the introduction by the US of an outward processing program under tariff items 806 and 807 in 1961.[10] This program proved to be a tremendous boon to Mexico. Originally aimed at facilitating intercorporate trade, combined with the Mexican program of in-bond processing – the Maquiladora program introduced in 1966 – it created a marriage made in heaven. "U.S. assembly activities in Mexico represent an important case of a mutually advantageous trading arrangement between two neighbours. Mexico needs to maintain an income flow from non-oil exports, and to increase employment opportunities in northern areas. The U.S. is helped to regain international competitiveness in industries that involve labor-intensive processes by taking advantage of low Mexican wages."[11] By 1989, the maquilas accounted for nearly half of Mexico's exports to the United States,[12] employing some 450,000 people in some 1,700 plants and taking the lion's share of US imports under the outward processing rules. In 1989, imports from Mexico under the program totaled US$12.5 billion and included, in order of importance: motor

---

[7]   United States International Trade Commission, *Review of Trade and Investment Liberalization Measures by Mexico and Prospects for Future United-States Mexican Relations* (Washington: USITC Publication 2275, April, 1990), pp. 2-6 to 2-7.

[8]   Nisso Bucay and Eduardo Perez Motta, "Trade Negotiation Strategy for Mexico," in John Whalley, ed., *The Small Among the Big* (London: Centre for the Study of International Economic Relations, 1988), p. 186.

[9]   See Table 4.4 in Sidney Weintraub, *A Marriage of Convenience: Relations Between Mexico and the United States* (New York: Oxford University Press, 1990), p. 76.

[10] Now tariff items 9801.00.60 and 9802.00.80 of the Harmonized Tariff System of Tariff Nomenclature introduced by the United States in 1989.

[11] Nisso Bucay and Eduardo Perez Motta, "Mexico," chapter 6 in John Whalley, ed., *Dealing with the North: Developing Countries and the Global Trading System* (London: Centre for the Study of International Economic Relations, 1987), p. 217.

[12] See Table 4.5 in Sidney Weintraub, *A Marriage of Convenience: Relations Between Mexico and the United States* (New York: Oxford University Press, 1990), p. 78.

vehicles, electrical conductors, televisions, motor vehicle parts, electrical circuits, combustion engines and textiles and apparel.[13]

As with Canada, a good deal of US-Mexico trade is intercorporate, not only as a result of the Maquiladora program but as a result of US investment in Mexico and, over the last few years, Mexican investment in the United States. Three-quarters of Mexico's manufactured exports are intermediate goods and most of them are traded between related companies.[14] In addition to the usual array of US corporate giants whose products now command worldwide recognition (Coca-Cola, IBM, Dupont, Ford and GM), smaller and lesser known companies have invested in either Maquiladora or more conventional branch plants.[15] In 1988, some 8,420 foreign companies operated in Mexico. By the end of 1989, US direct foreign investment stood at nearly US $17 billion representing some 63 percent of all FDI in Mexico.[16] In addition, large Mexican corporations such as Cementos Mexicanos have begun to invest in the United States in order to facilitate their penetration of the American market.

The development of much closer trade and investment ties over the past few years has now created the basis for a potentially successful free-trade negotiation.[17] On both sides of the border, there are now stake holders in a successful

---

13 United States International Trade Commission, *Review of Trade and Investment Liberalization Measures by Mexico and Prospects for Future United-States Mexican Relations* (Washington: USITC Publication 2275, April, 1990), pp. 5-13 to 5-14.

14 Sidney Weintraub, "The Impact of the Agreement [the Canada-US FTA] on Mexico" in Peter Morici, ed., *Making Free Trade Work* (New York: Council on Foreign Relations, 1990), fn. 8.

15 Sidney Weintraub in "The North American Free Trade Debate," paper prepared for the International Forum: Mexico's Trade Options in the Changing International Economy, Universidad Tecnologica de Mexico, Mexico City, June 11-15, 1990 notes that over the past decade Mexico and the United States "have silently integrated" as a result of the influx of US-based multinationals into Mexico. This has been a relatively recent phenomenon. In their initial search for low-cost manufacturing sites to complement their US operations, US manufacturers ignored much of Latin America, convinced that the legacy of hostile governments, un-skilled labour forces, political instability, low productivity and lack of control as a result of investment restrictions made such investments unprofitable. This is now changing as Latin America changes. American corporations prefer Mexico and similar locations because they are closer to home. Thus US multinationals are at the forefront of calls to create an integrated regional market.

16 United States International Trade Commission, *Review of Trade and Investment Liberalization Measures by Mexico and Prospects for Future United-States Mexican Relations* (Washington: USITC Publication 2275, April, 1990), p. 5-2.

17 Sidney Weintraub in *Mexican Trade Policy and the North American Community* (Washington: Center for Strategic and International Studies, 1988) discusses the changing politics of bilateral trade in the United States and Mexico, pp. 22-26.

outcome.[18] For American industry, an agreement that provides guaranteed access for foreign investment, protects intellectual property, places energy trade on a market footing and enhances access for US capital equipment and high technology products would offset the challenge of greater competition from lower-cost Mexican manufactures. For Mexican industry, an agreement that gave it both free and more secure access and a better way to deal with the myriad of disputes that arise in a complex trade and investment relationship would be welcome and would at the same time give it much greater assurance that the current, market-oriented, outward-looking trade regime would stay in place.[19]

Canada-Mexico Trade Relations

By way of contrast, trade and investment relations between Canada and Mexico can be described as rudimentary at best. Total two-way trade reached C$2.3 billion in 1989 with Mexican exports approximately twice those of Canada. Canadian exports were divided chiefly among food and live animals, manufactured goods and machinery and transportation equipment, while those of Mexico were heavily concentrated in machinery and transportation equipment (see table 9). Given the heavy concentration in automotive trade and in other machinery and equipment involving US-based multinationals, it is probable that the trade figures are significantly underreported as a result of transshipment through the United States. Even so, bilateral trade with Mexico rates below bilateral trade with Japan, the EC, the Asian NICs, the PRC and the USSR (see table 10). The level of Canadian investment in Mexico is similarly low. The total stock of direct Canadian investment in 1990 is less than half a billion dollars and is concentrated

---

[18] The presence of such stakeholders is well illustrated in the report of a binational commission of private sector individuals which recommended in 1989 that the United States and Mexico move rapidly to negotiate free trade in as many sectors as possible. See Bilateral Commission on the Future of United-States Mexican Relations, *The Challenge of Interdependence: Mexico and the United States* (New York: University Press of America, 1989).

[19] One of the greatest problems facing Mexican industrialists has been the lack of continuity and predictability in Mexican trade and industrial policy. Note Nisso Bucay and Eduardo Perez Motta: "... in each decade of the last 40 years there have been wide fluctuations in the use of trade policies for balance of payment purposes. Cumulatively this has sent a strong signal to both producers and consumers in Mexico that any trade policy strategy is temporary. What may be expected in the way of resource reallocation from any announced trade policy has not typically been realized because of this problem of credibility. On the contrary, trade liberalization tends to yield once-and-for-all gains, and investors do not shift resources toward export sectors, because of the expectation that the latest policy will likely be reversed." "Mexico," chapter 6 in John Whalley, ed., *Dealing with the North: Developing Countries and the Global Trading System* (London: Centre for the Study of International Economic Relations, 1987), p. 225.

in mining.[20] The most important economic relationship between Canada and Mexico involves tourism with the balance heavily in Mexico's favour.

Given the historic insignificance of trade and investment between the two countries, it is not surprising that the instruments for managing the relationship have never become very sophisticated. Canada and Mexico signed a Commercial Agreement in 1946 which provided for the exchange of most-favoured-nation status and little else. This agreement was considered sufficient until the late 1970s when Mexico's perceived importance as an oil-rich country led to increased Canadian interest in trade and investment ties. In 1980 the two countries signed an Agreement on Industrial and Energy Cooperation which called for technical cooperation paving the way for greater efforts by Canadian industry and government to penetrate the Mexican economy. Mexico looked forward to becoming the principal supplier of oil for Canada's eastern provinces while Canada dreamed of selling Candu reactors for Mexico's ambitious rural electrification program. The collapse of the Mexican economy in 1982 brought these efforts to a halt before much had been achieved.[21] A 1984 Commercial Agreement sought to revive interest but with little practical result. Mexico's accession to GATT in 1986 in effect superseded the previous bilateral instruments but again led to little new trade or investment.

Table 9
Canadian Merchandise Trade with Mexico

	1988		1989	
	Exports	Imports	Exports	Imports
		(Thousands of Cdn. dollars)		
Food and live animals	157,845	112,206	150,336	112,354
Beverages and Tobacco	307	12,596	223	15,363
Crude materials, inedible, exc. fuel	48,547	69,172	45,220	23,295
Mineral fuels, lubrcnts, related matr.	2,886	59,753	38	49,406
Oils and fats, animal & vegetable	1,827	--	1,741	--
Chemicals and related products	18,872	13,505	7,668	13,845
Manufactured goods by chief material	117,261	191,064	161,829	332,104
Machinery and transport equipment	129,798	828,706	213,830	1,100,863
Miscellaneous mfrd. artcls, nspf	3,954	29,965	4,769	42,381
Articles not provided for elsewhere	7,662	10,716	17,397	8,718
Total	489,002	1,327,726	603,098	1,698,368

Source: See table 8

---

[20] *Maclean's*, March 26, 1990, p. 46. The total in 1988 was US$ 323.5 million, accounting for 1.3 percent of direct foreign investment in Mexico, ranking Canada as ninth among foreign investors in Mexico. Figures supplied by SECOFI and the Mexican Embassy.

[21] Gabriel Székely, "Dilemmas of Export Diversification in a Developing Economy: Mexican Oil in the 1980s," *World Development*, vol. 17, no 11 (November, 1989), pp. 1789-1790.

Things are, however, changing rapidly. A new era was ushered in with a flourish in January of 1990 when seven Mexican Cabinet Secretaries descended on Ottawa on a trade and investment mission.[22] This was followed in March by an official visit by Prime Minister Mulroney at which time he and President Salinas signed some ten separate agreements, including a framework agreement to bolster trade and investment ties. The Prime Minister noted that "these [10] agreements constitute the action-plan and backbone of a new partnership."[23] International Trade Minister John Crosbie followed up with a trade mission to Mexico in April while Commerce Secretary Serra made a quick visit to Montreal following the Salinas-Bush meeting in Washington in June, to brief Crosbie on the outcome of these US-Mexico discussions and review possible Canadian participation.

Table 10
Geographic Distribution of Canadian Merchandise Trade
(percent)

	1988		1989	
Trading Partner	Exports	Imports	Exports	Imports
United States	73.0	65.7	73.3	65.2
Mexico	0.4	1.0	0.5	1.3
EC	8.0	12.2	8.5	11.1
Japan	6.5	7.0	6.5	7.1
Other Latin America	1.4	2.0	1.1	2.1
Rest of World	10.8	12.0	10.1	13.3

Source: Statistics Canada, catalogues 65202 and 65203 for 1988 and 1989. Totals may not add due to rounding.

To underline that these government-to-government meetings reflect a changing commercial reality, Canadian business leaders have started building contacts and gaining contracts. Larry Thibeault, President of the CMA, led a private sector mission to Mexico in March and came away convinced that Canadians could and should do much more in Mexico.[24] Northern Telecom and Spar Aerospace recently landed $28 million and $20 million contracts respectively to participate in the first stages of the massive rebuilding of the Mexican telephone system.[25] Spar is now looking to expand its contract by supplying a communications satellite and two satellite control centres worth some C$130-170 million.[26] Canadian

---

[22] For a detailed report on this visit, see the report by Fred Blazer in *The Financial Post*, January 25, 1990.

[23] Quoted in *The Financial Post*, March 19, 1990.

[24] See the report on the mission by participant Fred Blazer in *The Financial Post*, March 22, 1990.

[25] *Maclean's*, March 26, 1990, p. 46.

[26] *Toronto Star*, March 11, 1990.

Airlines is re-introducing its Toronto-Mexico City scheduled service convinced there will be enough business traffic to make a profit.[27] Even so, these commercial contacts are starting from a very low base and have a long way to go.

If the Mexican market held only limited appeal for American companies in the 1960s and 1970s, it was of even more limited interest to Canadian companies. Distance alone proved a powerful deterrent. The traditional low level of trade between Canada and Mexico cannot be attributed primarily to the presence of tariff and other trade barriers in Canada nor will the removal of these trade barriers swamp Canada with low-cost goods. Canada's 5 or 10 percent tariff is not deterring imports of goods benefitting from significantly lower labour costs from Mexico. Rather, it is the absence of historic trade and investment ties and weak institutional links that have deterred more trade. Lack of Canadian interest was reinforced by the uncompetitiveness of Mexican industry and the limited opportunities available in the highly protected Mexican economy. Finally, few Canadian branch plants had mandates to penetrate the Mexican economy.

Table 11
Canadian Merchandise Trade with the United States

	1988		1989	
	Exports	Imports	Exports	Imports
		(Thousands of Cdn. dollars)		
Food and live animals	3,905,533	3,815,036	3,906,107	3,799,757
Beverages and Tobacco	507,061	507,061	483,921	483,921
Crude materials, inedible, exc. fuel	1,224,051	1,089,053	1,202,346	1,082,510
Mineral fuels, lubrcnts, related matr.	10,212,588	1,637,801	10,283,179	2,015,345
Oils and fats, animal & vegetable	105,592	90,497	92,386	106,350
Chemicals and related products	4,026,639	4,225,446	3,908,337	4,682,458
Manufactured goods by chief material	30,065,452	17,303,184	28,593,063	18,441,842
Machinery and transport equipment	44,829,089	52,404,949	45,615,459	51,324,466
Miscellaneous mfrd. artcls, nspf	2,021,131	3,861,908	2,128,079	4,468,576
Articles not provided for elsewhere	633,252	1,814,237	1,672,101	1,784,491
Total	97,530,434	86,020,888	97,930,006	87,914,295

Source: See table 8.

The changes that can come about over the next few years, however, can be illustrated by what is happening in the automotive sector. Both the Big Three and their suppliers are increasing their investment in Mexico to take advantage of lower cost labour and thus lay the foundation for increased trade. The Big Three

---

[27] Interview with PWA executive. Canada-Mexico tourist traffic is carried almost exclusively by charter. Business travellers in Eastern Canada interested in Mexico have to fly either through Dallas with American Airlines or from Mirabel with Iberia. From Western Canada, the most common route is through Los Angeles.

are bringing Mexican parts into Canada duty-free under the terms of the Autopact. Japanese assemblers in Canada are paying the 6.2 percent GPT on their Mexican imports. A new Mexican accord would make little difference to these emerging patterns. As the Mexican economy develops due to internal reforms, Canadians will experience greater competition both in terms of goods and in terms of attracting investment capital. That is a reality with which we must come to terms regardless of whether Mexico negotiates a free-trade agreement with the United States, joins the FTA or enters into some other trilateral arrangement.[28]

It is the combined effect of US interest in Mexico and Mexico's unilateral program of reform, therefore, that has slowly rekindled Canadian interest in a more active trade and economic partnership. That interest has greatly accelerated as a result of the prospect of a US-Mexico agreement, motivated as much by concern about the impact of such an agreement on Canadian interests in the United States as by Canada-Mexico trade and investment potential.

Canada-US-Mexico Trade and Investment

Mexico and Canada are in many ways competitors in the US market. That competition may increase as manufacturers in both countries gear up to take advantage of improved trading conditions. The US is the largest trading partner for both Mexico and Canada, taking roughly 70 percent of each country's exports and supplying approximately the same proportion of their imports. Relative Mexican and Canadian shares of the US import market have remained fairly constant over the last decade (around 6 percent for Mexico and 20 percent for Canada), but both countries' shares of fully manufactured products have steadily increased. As indicated in table 12, both countries are intensifying trade in the same sectors: power generating equipment, transportation, telecommunications equipment and other machinery and equipment sectors. Between 1979 and 1987,

---

[28] James P. Womack, "North American Integration in the Motor Vehicle Sector: Logic and Consequences," paper prepared for the International Forum: Mexico's Trade Options in the Changing International Economy, Universidad Tecnologica de Mexico, Mexico City, June 11-15, 1990 provides a detailed analysis of the impact on the auto industry of further North American integration. He forecasts new investment and consolidation by the Big Three and the major Asian transplants based on an integrated North American market. As Mexican workers and production become reliable and the Mexican market expands, Mexico will be made part of a more integrated North American market and production unit. He argues that on the basis of current trends, Mexico will be assigned responsibility for the production of entry-level vehicles (parts and assembly) and some labour-intensive parts, while production of mid-sized and luxury vehicles will be further consolidated in the mid-West and Ontario based on the techniques of flexible (just-in-time) manufacturing pioneered by the Japanese but now being adapted in North America. The main losers will be entry-level builders in Asia and traditional Mexican producers.

the proportion of Canada's exports to the United States made up of machinery and transport equipment rose from 34 percent to 43 percent of the total. During the same period, Mexico's share doubled from 21 to 42 percent, although in absolute terms Canada remains a much more important supplier.

Given the greater proximity of US manufacturers to the Mexican market and their greater investment commitments (nearly $17 billion in direct investment), the US share of the Mexican import market far outstrips that of Canada. Many more US-based companies have production or manufacturing operations in Mexico. Just as in the case of US-Canada trade, much US-Mexican trade is between related parties. Table 8 indicates the much greater extent to which US manufacturers have penetrated the Mexican market.

Of Mexico's $340 million in exports to Canada in 1980, a fraction were manufactured products. In the same year, a third of Canada's $485 million in exports to Mexico were manufactured products. By 1989, two-thirds of Canada's exports to Mexico ($433 million) were manufactured products, whereas nine of Mexico's top ten export sectors to Canada, representing 78 percent of a total of $1.7 billion, were manufactured goods (i.e., auto parts $315 million; telecommunications $164 million; office machines $132 million; and computers $132 million).

Table 12
The Distribution of US Merchandise Imports from Canada and Mexico
(percent)

	1979		1987	
Sector	Canada	Mexico	Canada	Mexico
Food and Live Animals	3.5	16.6	4.3	10.2
Beverages and Tobacco	0.9	0.9	0.7	1.4
Crude Materials, Inedible	15.9	3.1	9.4	1.9
Mineral Fuels	14.3	35.2	9.6	19.4
Edible Oils, Fats, Waxes	-	-	0.1	-
Chemicals	6.4	2.2	4.3	2.0
Manufactured Goods	19.0	9.9	19.0	10.2
Machinery and Transport	34.2	21.0	43.4	42.6
Miscellaneous Manufactures	2.7	7.9	4.8	8.6
Miscellaneous Transactions	3.1	3.2	4.4	3.7

Source: Adapted from *Peter Morici, Life After Free Trade: U.S.-Canadian Commercial Relations in the 1990s*, Table 3 (Halifax: Institute for Research on Public Policy, forthcoming).

The fact that Canadian and Mexican manufacturers compete for the same broad market segments may be of some concern to individual firms, particularly labour-intensive firms. It should not necessarily be of concern at an aggregate level. International trade has moved well beyond the classic paradigm of wool for wine. Trade is now as much intra-firm as interfirm and countries sell each other a much wider range of products within broad sectors. An increasing proportion of modern trade is in components of more sophisticated products. While Canadian comparative advantage continues to lie in resources and resource-based products, an increasing proportion of Canadian trade is in semi-finished goods, i.e., in producer goods, components and subassemblies. Mexico, with an abundance of low-cost labour, and a smaller endowment of resources, enjoys a comparative advantage in assembly operations and in labour-intensive manufacturing. Thus, while Canada and Mexico may compete in the same broad industrial sectors, each is developing expertise and excellence in different segments (e.g., price and quality) of the same sub-sectors or in related sub-sectors. In short, the challenge of the new competition from Mexico, much of which will benefit the Canadian economy in the long run, should not be exaggerated.

Too much has been made of the labour-cost advantage enjoyed by Mexico as a threat to competing production in the United States and Canada. There is no question that Mexican hourly labour rates are significantly lower than those in Canada and the United States. At least four factors, however, mitigate this advantage. In the first place, Mexican labour is in many instances not very productive. Most Mexican labour is unskilled or semi-skilled and not as disciplined and trained as labour in Canada and the United States. For example, the Nissan plant in Cuernavaca takes more than twice as long to produce a car as the Nissan plant in Tennessee.[29] Secondly, labour as a percentage of production costs is steadily declining in most industries. The combined effect of more sophisticated machinery and more computer-aided design and production has reduced the importance of labour costs in determining plant location. Thirdly, the quality of the Mexican infrastructure – particularly transportation and communications – remains very low. Finally, other factors, such as proximity to and reliability of suppliers and closeness to final markets are more important factors in plant location today than labour costs, particularly as flexible manufacturing techniques take hold in North America. These factors offset much of Mexico's labour-cost advantage in many industries. As the Mexican economy develops and overcomes these disadvantages, its labour-cost advantage will also gradually disappear. Thus the labour-cost advantage is at best a transitory phenomenon of significance to a limited number of products. Indeed, as Mexican production moves up the value-added ladder, Mexico is likely to become a more formidable competitor than it is now.[30]

---

29 Fred Blazer, *The Financial Post,* March 22, 1990.

30 These issues are discussed in detail, with references to ongoing research, by James P. Womack, "North American Integration in the Motor Vehicle Sector: Logic and Consequences," and Michael J. Piore, "Mexican Social Standards and U.S. Business Strategy in an Integrated North American Market," papers prepared for the International Forum: Mexico's

The emerging patterns of US-Mexico and US-Canada trade should thus neither excite undue anxiety nor offer room for complacency; they do suggest that a
significant number of Canadian companies are likely to be affected by a Mexico-
US agreement through their contracts with US suppliers, customers, owners, li-
censees and distributors. Canadian companies would face greater competition
from their US competitors if the latter were able to source some of their components more cheaply in Mexico. The greater integration of Mexican and US companies resulting from a bilateral accord as well as greater integration of Canadian
and US companies that the FTA is encouraging will place US companies in a
strategic position to exploit increased opportunities in all three markets while
Canadian companies remain limited to only two. In addition, Canadian companies may see some erosion of the preferences resulting from the FTA as Mexican
companies enjoy similar or even better access conditions.

Chart 4
Per Capita Imports for the US, Canada and Mexico, 1986

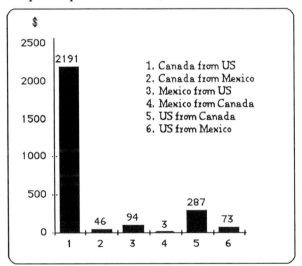

Source: Sidney Weintraub, *Mexican Trade Policy and the North
American Community,* p. 34.

An agreement limited to the United States and Mexico could undermine
Canada's ability to attract new investment, particularly foreign investment. Few
Canadian companies are likely to relocate to Mexico – of the nearly 1700 firms in

Trade Options in the Changing International Economy, Universidad Tecnologica de Mexico,
Mexico City, June 11-15, 1990.

Mexico's Maquiladora operations, only a few are Canadian.[31] We are more likely to see the diversion of new foreign investment to Mexico which in the absence of a Mexico-US agreement might have located in Canada.

As hosts to many branch-plant operations, Canada and Mexico rely heavily on foreign (largely US) investment capital and technology. In 1989, the total stock of foreign investment in Canada approached $110 billion, of which close to 70 percent was controlled by US-based companies.[32] Total foreign investment in Mexico in 1989 amounted to close to $27 billion, of which about 63 percent was of US origin.[33] Canada and Mexico have embarked on economic development strategies that seek to attract new foreign investment on the basis of secure access to the US market. Canadian investment missions across the Atlantic and Pacific have emphasized the privileged access European and Japanese transplants would enjoy in the US market from a base in Canada. Missions to the United States have portrayed Canada as an attractive alternative to many US states while guaranteeing equivalent access. A bilateral agreement between the United States and Mexico which provided access to the US for Mexican-based manufacturers on a similar basis to that of Canadian-based manufacturers, and at the same time provided assured safeguards to US investment capital, could significantly undermine Canada's ability to attract new foreign, particularly US, investment. This effect would be of much less significance if the free-trade accord were to be tripartite.

Given the already highly integrated nature of Canada-US business and US-Mexico business, a separate agreement between the US and Mexico along lines similar to the FTA is likely to complicate ongoing trade and investment. US and Canadian companies already complain about the complexities of the FTA and will complain even more if a new and different set of rules is developed for trade with Mexico. Even if Canada is not involved, these rules will have an impact on Canadian trade, for example, as US customers or suppliers factor in whether they want to satisfy the US-Mexico or US-Canada rules of origin. New US investment in Canada or Mexico will not aim at satisfying the Canadian or Mexican markets; rather, it must fit into the global strategies of these companies to serve wider markets. Rules that frustrate flexibility in making production and investment

---

[31] A few autoparts manufacturers have set up maquilas, including Fleck Manufacturing, Bendix Safety Restraints and Custom Trim. See *The Financial Times of Canada*, April 2, 1990. The combined effect of distance and the absence of a Canadian equivalent of the US outward-processing program make maquilas less attractive for Canadian manufacturers.

[32] Bank of Canada Review, May 1990.

[33] US International Trade Commission, *Review of Trade and Investment Liberalization Measures by Mexico and Prospect for Future United States-Mexican Relations*, Publication 2275 of April, 1990, pp. 5-1, 5-2.

decisions will be resisted and will undermine the restructuring that a free-trade agreement is meant to foster.

While a bilateral US-Mexico accord would adversely affect Canadian trade and investment interests, Canadian participation in an integrated North American market should on balance have positive effects. It would allow companies to develop production and marketing plans based on exploiting the comparative advantages of all three countries in servicing a market of some 360 million consumers. The resulting dynamic adjustment should benefit all three countries. For example, American food processors are likely to invest in processing facilities in Mexico to take advantage of low labour costs and a ready supply of raw materials suited to canning and freezing. This would release higher quality produce from the American sunbelt for the fresh market, thus increasing choice and lowering costs for consumers throughout North America.

More generally, rationalization and restructuring should increase the ability of North American firms to meet global competition. A thriving Mexican economy would provide these companies with an improved platform from which to market their goods and services to the rest of Latin America. Again, at its most practical, businesses in all three countries would welcome common rules of origin, particularly if these are an improved version of what is currently to be found in the FTA.

If Mexico's domestic economic reforms work and a Mexico-Canada-US FTA is negotiated, Canadian entrepreneurs will find Mexico to be a very attractive new market, and they will be able to count on the necessary institutional and structural links to help them exploit that market. In sum, a tripartite arrangement can help prevent the diversion of trade and investment that might result from a bilateral US-Mexico accord and at the same time provide new trade and investment opportunities.

5

Issues and Options
for the Future

On the basis of the foregoing analysis, there appear to be significant trade and economic reasons to buttress the geopolitical reasons for Canada to consider joining the United States and Mexico in the negotiation of a North American Free Trade Agreement. What then are the available options?

The conventional answer in both Canada and the United States until recently would have been to await results in the latest round of multilateral trade negotiations (MTN) held under the auspices of the GATT – the Uruguay Round – before taking any precipitous decisions. It is still a good answer but perhaps no longer a sufficient answer. The current round, launched with much difficulty in September of 1986 and labouring to a scheduled conclusion at the end of 1990, may well address some of the issues of immediate concern to Canada, the United States and Mexico and reduce the urgency or complexity of any bilateral or trilateral discussions. At the same time, it would be naive to expect the Uruguay Round to make such breakthroughs as to obviate the attraction of a North American accord. As an alternative, the Uruguay Round, with its complex agenda and many participants, is unlikely to prove satisfactory. Rather, it should be regarded as a precursor to more intense bilateral or trilateral discussions which could be initiated following the conclusion of the round. A pragmatic approach, therefore, suggests that there is little to be gained by rushing to initiate bilateral or trilateral discussions before 1991; instead, the breathing spell offered by the Uruguay Round can be used to take a serious look at what would be involved in negotiations with Mexico and to continue preparatory studies and discussions.

The outcome of the 1990 Economic Summit held in Houston in July suggests that the results of the MTN may be broad but shallow with the critical issue of farm subsidies continuing to bedevil a deeper consensus on other issues. While the remaining months of the Uruguay Round should fully occupy most negotiating energy and resources, this should not preclude serious consideration of the supplementary opportunities offered by bilateral or trilateral alternatives.[1]

It should be stressed that bilateral negotiations should be seen as a complement rather than as an alternative to multilateral negotiations. Having joined GATT, Mexico has affirmed that it believes that universal solutions are better than particular ones. Like Canada and the United States, it has accepted that some issues can only be resolved multilaterally while others can best be solved multilaterally. Nevertheless, the multilateral system provides for bilateral negotiations because sometimes far-reaching results can only be achieved on a less than universal basis. The challenge is to find the right balance between multilateral and bilateral negotiations. From this perspective, the more successful the outcome of the Uruguay Round, the less pressure there will be on Mexican leaders to find regional solutions. However, should the Uruguay Round results be broad but shallow, then the regional option will take on increased urgency.[2]

It would be disingenuous to insist that a tripartite arrangment involving Canada, the United States and Mexico would not soften their support for multilateralism. But one must not confuse ends and means. The purpose of international trade agreements is to facilitate trade and thereby increase national and international welfare. They do not exist for their own sake. By entering into their bilateral FTA, Canada and the United States recognized that the GATT could not be expected to resolve all bilateral trade and economic problems between them. There are many unique aspects of the Canada-US relationship that the GATT process had been unable to address and which were successfully resolved by the FTA. Insisting that they could only be addressed multilaterally would have been

---

[1]   See news reports in *The Toronto Globe and Mail* and *The New York Times* for July 8-11, 1990.

[2]   See Murray Smith, "Canada, Mexico and the United States: Pursuing Common Multilateral Interests and Exploring North American Options," and Jeffrey Schott, "A Strategy for Mexican Trade Policy in the 1990s," papers prepared for the International Forum: Mexico's Trade Options in the Changing International Economy, Universidad Tecnologica de Mexico, Mexico City, June 11-15, 1990 for discussion of the relationship between the Uruguay Round negotiations and US-Mexico or Canada-US-Mexico negotiations.

to insist that they not be resolved, to the detriment not only of Canadian and US entrepreneurs but also of the multilateral system itself.[3] The governments that drew up the GATT more than forty years ago stipulated that discriminatory regional arrangements were acceptable as long as they led to increased world trade. Geography as well as a high degree of integration among business and capital markets made a Canada-US free trade agreement an intelligent choice and now suggests that extending the agreement to Mexico is the next logical step.[4]

In considering regional complements to GATT, it is difficult to take an agreement limited to Canada and Mexico seriously. Both bilateral trade and investment are embryonic and would hardly warrant the necessary investment in resources and political will. While the potential for bilateral trade and investment may be much greater, it is unlikely to be realized soon or to be immediately affected by a bilateral accord. Mexican accession to the GATT in 1986 removed the principal Canadian interest in a bilateral treaty with binding commitments.

Some observers have suggested that the United States and Mexico should conclude an accord similar to that between the United States and Canada and then the three countries should negotiate appropriate crosswalk provisions between the two agreements. Indeed, some have suggested, particularly in view of the ascendancy of bilateralism in Washington, that the United States might well negotiate a series of such parallel accords. In effect, the United States would end up as the hub connecting a series of free-trade agreements. Such an approach would not be in Canada's interest and probably not in the interest of either Mexico or the United States. It would retard development of an integrated North American market and make it too easy for the United States to play Canada and Mexico and any other spoke nations off against each other in arrangements inimical to their interests. Although a series of reciprocal, self-balancing agreements may hold some attraction for mercantilists, these could prove seriously destructive of the open, multilateral trading system. While regional arrangements such

---

3   The issue is discussed in more detail in the final chapters of the revised edition of W. F. Stone, *Canada, the GATT and the International Trading System*, forthcoming from the Institute for Research on Public Policy. William Diebold has also written a thoughtful essay on the conflict between bilateralism and multilateralism well worth a careful reading. See his *Bilateralism, Multilateralism and Canada in U.S. Trade Policy* (New York; Council on Foreign Relations, 1988).

4   See Jeffrey J. Schott, ed., *Free Trade Areas and U.S. Trade Policy* (Washington: Institute for International Economics, 1989) and Peter Morici, ed., *Making Free Trade Work* (New York: Council on Foreign Relations, 1990) both of which consider the likelihood of the United States entering into more free trade areas, particularly with Mexico, and the implication of such agreements for the future evolution of the GATT and US trade policy.

as the Canada-US FTA can be complementary to GATT, the hub and spoke approach would place serious strains on the system.[5]

In effect, therefore, should Canada indicate any interest in a North American free-trade accord, the most sensible option would be to trilateralize the negotiations. There are, of course, variants on what this would involve ranging from trilateralizing the FTA to the negotiation of an entirely new agreement. For analytical purposes, however, it is sufficient to examine the general and specific issues that would be raised should Canada, the United States and Mexico proceed to negotiate some kind of tripartite arrangement without worrying at this stage about the form such an arrangement should take.

The Trilateral Option

In considering the strategic implications of a tripartite free-trade arrangement, we must retain a sense of proportion. Heightened awareness of trade policy issues resulting from the 1988 FTA debate has resulted in both unrealistic expectations and far-fetched fears. Trade policy and trade measures are no more than a few of the weapons in the arsenal of policies and measures available to governments to influence economic performance. Trade policy is largely a matter of solving problems within a framework of domestic and international rules as well as competing domestic and international political and economic pressures. Ultimately, the solutions to these problems should increase national and international welfare. To achieve that end, trade policy pursues three basic objectives:

- access – improving access to foreign markets by reducing or eliminating barriers imposed by foreign governments to imports;
- adjustment – inducing the domestic economy to become more competitive by exposing it to international competition and integrating it into the larger world economy; and
- systemic – establishing and preserving an effective trade relations system based on the rule of law and the principle of non-discrimination.

The first of these is a business objective that seeks to maximize export and profit opportunities for domestic producers already able to compete on the inter-

---

[5]   See C. Michael Aho and Sylvia Ostry, "Regional Trading Blocks: Pragmatic or Problematic Policy," in William E. Brock and Robert D. Hormats, eds., *The Global Economy: America's Role in the Decade Ahead* (New York: the American Assembly, 1990) for a critical examination of the subtle attraction of regionalism. Ron Wonnacott's presentation at the International Forum: Mexico's Trade Options in the Changing International Economy, Universidad Tecnologica de Mexico, Mexico City, June 11-15, 1990 also provides a strong antidote against parallel accords. I am indebted to Professor Wonnacott for the hub and spoke metaphor.

national market. The second is an economic objective based on the ideas of classic economic trade theory. The third is primarily a political and bureaucratic objective and is grounded in the values of international law; its successful pursuit maintains the vehicle for fulfilling the other two.[6]

By pursuing these three objectives, trade policy seeks directly to influence the extent and nature of a country's foreign trade and indirectly a country's economic development. Historically, trade policy has been the primary instrument used by Canadian governments to guide economic development. The extent to which trade policy can have this influence, however, can be easily exaggerated, although political debate would sometimes suggest otherwise.[7] Generally speaking, minor changes in the deployment of trade policy instruments will lead to minor changes in exports or imports or industrial activity while major changes may lead to more substantial changes. Over the years, most changes have been small and incremental, despite claims to the contrary. Their overall economic effect has been small, although they may be more profound at the level of the firm.

Viewed from this perspective, the FTA did not constitute any radical changes. Too much has been made of the substantive provisions of the FTA by both its critics and its proponents. What counted in the end was its psychological impact, and much of that was achieved prior to and during the negotiations. The actual

---

[6] The analysis presented here proceeds from the assumptions of classical international trade theory. These assumptions are not shared by all analysts. In *The Political Economy of International Relations* (Princeton: Princeton University Press, 1987), Robert Gilpin describes the other two basic theoretical frameworks as Marxism and Nationalism. For purposes of this study, Marxist analysis need not be taken too seriously. More difficult are the claims of the Nationalist school of analysts who have tried to provide old-fashioned mercantilism with a more sophisticated creed. It is their views that find much popular favour and underpin skepticism about markets and the benefits of trade liberalization (pp. 25-64 and 172-190). In addition, modern theoretical arguments have sought to give some credence to the economic value of discrimination. While further study and reflection have debunked some of the wilder claims of "strategic trade policy", these theories have forced economists to re-examine some of the most entrenched and respected economic theories and to test their continuing validity. Many economists have been prepared to accept that there may be theoretical instances where subsidies and other forms of intervention would lead to improved net economic welfare, but that the circumstances are so rare as to make the theory virtually inapplicable to policy. For a discussion of these new theories, see Richard G. Lipsey and Wendy Dobson, *Shaping Comparative Advantage* (Toronto: C.D. Howe Institute, 1987) and Klaus Stegemann, "Policy Rivalry Among Industrial States: What can we learn from Models of Strategic Trade Policy?" *International Organization,* vol. 43, no. 1 (Winter, 1989), pp. 73-100.

[7] Public debate, particularly in the House of Commons, sometimes suggests that any reduction in the tariff or quota protecting, for example, clothing producers or ice cream and yoghurt producers, will bring these industries to their knees. Experience indicates that only very major changes have this kind of impact.

agreement and its implementing legislation did little more than provide a more secure basis for consolidating the changed attitude of Canadian business to the international economy and Canada's place in it. Practical or concrete changes required of governments by the FTA were relatively minor. Modelling of the anticipated economic impact of the FTA underscores this point. Overall changes in GNP and employment in the order of 2 to 2.5 percent over ten years were predicted by the econometric analyses of the Department of Finance and the Economic Council of Canada.[8] In other words, the major impact of the FTA was not substantive but symbolic marking a revolution in attitudes rather than in laws and regulations.

The anticipated effects of a US-Mexico agreement or a trilateral accord should be viewed in this light. First of all, its effects should not be confused with the impact of events already requiring adjustment in the Canadian economy. Adjustment to the Canada-US FTA, to the effects of previous multilateral rounds and to the globalization of the economy through the much freer flow of capital and investment and accelerating technological change should not be confused with adjustment to a new agreement. Furthermore, it should be appreciated that Canadian industry is already adapting to some extent to Mexico's unilateral program of reforms to its economy. Additional factors introduced by a tripartite accord would thus need to be distinguished from existing adjustment pressures, not an easy task given the myriad of forces that buffet any modern economy.

As the issues are publicly debated, the effect of these other forces will not be clearly appreciated by many Canadians trying to assess the impact of yet another change in trading circumstances. The major controversies that will be generated by a decision to negotiate a North American free-trade agreement, therefore, will involve political perceptions more than specific trade and economic issues. In addition to fears about competing with low-cost Mexican labour, they will involve suspicion that Canada is being used to give legitimacy to a corrupt administration in Mexico; anxiety about the erosion of Canadian identity as Canada becomes ever more closely tied economically to the United States; and worry that the US will wring more concessions from Canada. To each of these fears, there is a sound but complex answer.

Mexico does enjoy lower labour costs; that is its comparative advantage allowing it to trade with countries with much more sophisticated but more costly labour forces. Lower labour costs make up to some extent for Mexico's much

---

[8]   The findings of the ECC are summarized in Economic Council of Canada, *Venturing Forth: An Assessment of the Canada-U.S. Trade Agreement* (Ottawa: Supply and Services, 1988). The Finance findings are in *The Canada-U.S. Free Trade Agreement: An Economic Assessment* (Ottawa: Department of Finance, 1988).

lower labour productivity, for its inadequate economic infrastructure, for its lack of quality industrial inputs, for its critical shortage of investment capital, for its scarce managerial talent, for its distance from major markets and for other critical economic factors. Those Canadians who insist that Mexico enjoys an unfair advantage because of its lower labour costs fail to appreciate what is involved in modern industrial organization and trade. It is Canadian industry that has most of the advantages. Only in a limited number of sectors does Mexico enjoy clear advantages and it is these sectors that will face the greatest need to adjust.

Suspicion about the legitimacy of the current Mexican Administration shows a similar parochial attitude. Putting aside the question of the many trade agreements Canada has already signed with other governments of more questionable reputation, the current Mexican administration offers the best hope for long-term democratic reforms. Mexico has been ruled for almost all of this century by one party which has been charged with a variety of crimes against democracy and human rights, many of which may well be true. One of the factors which helped the Institutional Revolutionary Party (PRI) maintain its long hold on the country was the degree of government interference required by the trade, investment and industrial policies of the past forty years. A high degree of government regulation breeds rent-holders interested in maintaining the status quo.[9] Not only have the economic reforms of the past five years swept these rent-holders to the side, but they have been accompanied by equally extensive political reforms.[10] A trilateral agreement that underwrites the current program of economic reform will also underwrite Mexico's political reforms.

Anxiety about Canadian identity attributes to trade and investment agreements a power and influence that they do not deserve. We live in a complex world requiring a whole host of intergovernmental agreements. Each of these represents, in some way, efforts to control and influence the gradual harmonization and homogenization of the international economy and the weakening of national differences. Modern transportation and communications have greatly in-

---

[9] Writes Sidney Weintraub: "A regime of import controls, discretionary decisions on the level of import protection, and case-by-case haggling over what Mexican can own what portion of some foreigner's direct investment, all promote their own forms of corruption. The more the market operates and the less the power of the government and officials to make economic decisions, the greater the likelihood of political freedom." in "The North American Free Trade Debate," paper prepared for the International Forum: Mexico's Trade Options in the Changing International Economy, Universidad Tecnologica de Mexico, Mexico City, June 11-15, 1990, pp. 13-14.

[10] See, for example, the *Maclean's* cover story for March 26, 1990 or Les Whittington in *The Ottawa Citizen* of March 10, 1990 for an account of the extensive political reforms being undertaken by Salinas in tandem with his economic reforms.

creased the pressure to harmonize while at the same time accentuating the desire for diversity. That is an ever-present conflict which governments must seek to resolve. That conflict is one of the pressures of modern economic life. Agreements do not alter these pressures; rather they respond to them and impose order where there would otherwise be chaos and conflict. Canadian identity is not a constant; it is a dynamic and ever-changing kaleidoscope of competing values and priorities responding to a wide range of influences. The impact of the Canada-US FTA is but one of those influences and expanding it to Mexico would change the nature of that influence somewhat. But it would be naive to think that without an FTA we would have been able to reduce the influence of American economic and other values affecting us from diverse directions. Similarly, including Mexico in that agreement will not alter the fact that as Mexico develops and becomes a more attractive place with which to do business, Canadians will be affected by Mexican cultural influences.

In the context of a trilateral negotiation, the United States will undoubtedly seek concessions from Canada that it was not able to gain during the initial negotiations. This is not a "bad" thing. The FTA was a win-win agreement, i.e., Canada and the United States traded concessions that, even if implemented unilaterally, would be to their mutual advantage. The need to view these as "concessions" is part of the ritual of international negotiations required to overcome political resistance to reducing the rents of powerful special interests. The 1987 agreement was not able to reach politically acceptable compromises on a number of issues, including the manner in which intellectual property rights are protected, barriers to government procurement contracts, subsidies to industrial activity, investment incentives and more. If, during the course of a US-Mexico-Canada negotiation some of these issues can be resolved, Canada will be one of the beneficiaries.

Ranked against the purveyors of these fears and anxieties will be business and academic commentators who are convinced that Canada should seize every opportunity to advance its trading interests and promote the development of a more competitive, outward-oriented economy. Typical is the attitude of York University economics Professor Ricardo Grinspun who wrote in January 1990:

> One point seems clear: an ostrich-like attitude on the part of Canada regarding increasing U.S.-Mexico integration would be detrimental. Canada's options need to be clarified and discussed. If the U.S.-Mexico negotiations are going to continue, then Canada should strive to be an active partner. A trilateral deal, or at least a Mexico-U.S. deal worked out

with active Canadian participation, would be much better than any separate U.S.-Mexico bilateral deal that leaves Canada out in the cold.[11]

Informetrica President Mike McCracken put it more bluntly: "Canada ought to get off its duff ... We'd better work on a bilateral agreement with the Mexicans or create a [North American] free trade area, or we'll only be able to trade with the U.S."[12]

In order to come to a realistic assessment of the problems that would arise in extending the FTA to Mexico, it is also necessary to differentiate between the very difficult problems of detail that will preoccupy the technicians from the more fundamental issues that will be the focus of political debate. Solving technical issues will require a tremendous amount of hard work, time and ingenuity but few negotiations founder on the shoals of technical detail. Solving political problems requires political will and statesmanship. Such problems arise more out of perceptions and fears than reality; they thrive on simplistic assumptions and naive assertions. Most negotiations that fail, fail because insufficient attention was paid to this dimension. If these problems can be solved by the statesmen, the technical issues will fall into place. Technical issues should not be allowed to drive negotiations and become stumbling blocks.

Complementary Objectives

Given the structure of Mexican trade and investment with the United States, Mexico can be expected to bring to any free-trade negotiations objectives and concerns very similar to those of Canada. These can be briefly summarized as follows:

- more open and secure access for its manufactures in order to underwrite continued domestic economic reform, boost investor confidence, attract more foreign capital and ensure sufficient technology transfer to allow Mexico to become more competitive on a global basis; its priority sectors include agriculture, textiles, clothing, automotive, steel and petrochemicals;
- an improved institutional basis for managing relations and settling disputes which would neutralize to some extent the disparities in power; and

---

11 Ricardo Grinspun, "Would a U.S.-Mexico FTA leave us economically jilted?" *Financial Times of Canada,* January 29, 1990. For more articles in the same vein, see Fred Blazer in *The Financial Post* of June 28 and July 5, 1990 and Peter Morton in *The Financial Post* of July 6, 1990.

12 *The Financial Post,* March 29, 1990.

- continuing freedom to deal with sensitive sectors such as energy, financial services and investment in order to meet delicate domestic priorities and leave room to manage nationalist opposition to an agreement.

Mexican and Canadian objectives are similar because they reflect the issues that naturally arise when a smaller economy is heavily dependent on trade with a large economy. While Mexico has turned its back on its protectionist past more recently than Canada, both countries look to a North American free-trade zone to underwrite domestic economic reform. In both countries, the agenda is largely driven by economic goals while the sensitivities are largely political. As a result, Canada and Mexico have a lot in common and, by joining forces, are more likely to achieve some of their objectives than by acting alone. This point has not been lost on US officials, a number of whom have suggested that the addition of Canada to the table would make the negotiations too complicated and undercut US ability to structure a "good" arrangement.

US objectives are not the same as those of Canada and Mexico, although they are not so different as to make an agreement impossible. As a global power, the US will bring concerns that range well beyond strictly bilateral issues. At the same time, given the nature of decision-making in Washington, US anxieties will sometimes seem very parochial. The United States believes that any agreement must not only satisfy its direct bilateral concerns but also advance its broader global trade agenda. While an agreement may respond to geopolitical impulses, it must also satisfy the very specific commercial interests of US business. These sometimes conflicting objectives translate into a grab bag of specific goals. The United States will want to:

- establish an agreement that will help to further underwrite the development of a market-oriented economy in Mexico and strengthen democracy;
- secure more open access for US providers of goods and services, not only in terms of border measures, but also in terms of domestic policies, such as subsidies and technical standards, and thus bring the Mexican trade and investment regime more into line with American ideology if not practice;
- ensure non-discriminatory and fair treatment of US investment and intellectual property rights;
- resolve individual irritants, although many of these have already been resolved over the period 1985-1990, paving the way for a constructive opening to broader negotiations;[13] and

---

[13] Tim Bennett, a former USTR official responsible for US-Mexico relations, argued in a paper presented at the International Forum: Mexico's Trade Options in the Changing International Economy, Universidad Tecnologica de Mexico, Mexico City, June 11-15, 1990, that the suc-

- develop rules and procedures to provide an improved basis for resolving trade and investment disputes with Mexico.

For the United States, while broad geopolitical considerations have proven critical in providing the necessary atmosphere in which negotiations can be launched, they will have to be buttressed by concrete trade and investment achievements if the agreement is to garner the necessary congressional support to be implemented in US domestic legislation. The political arithmetic in the United States Congress requires that any agreement must respond positively to the needs of more specific US interest groups than are alienated by it.

While Canada and Mexico share some basic objectives, the United States and Canada share many fundamental attitudes and experiences that have traditionally ensured that Canadian and American approaches are complementary. It was this shared background that in the end enabled the successful conclusion of the 1985-87 negotiations. The United States and Canada share a similar level of economic development, analogous economic and legal institutions, kindred political cultures and approaches to industrial policy, a highly integrated industrial structure as well as fifty years experience in negotiating antecedents to the FTA, including the 1935 and 1938 bilateral agreements and the GATT.[14] Mexico shares none of these elements, making bilateral negotiations between the United States and Mexico more difficult than the Canada-US negotiations. The addition of Canada to the table, therefore, should facilitate negotiations by broadening the basis for agreement among all three countries.

What Mexico (and Canada) Should Learn from the FTA Experience

As Canada discovered during its bilateral negotiations, negotiating with the United States on a one-on-one basis is not an easy task. The United States is a global power and as a result pursues its priorities in a manner that its close neighbours find hard to appreciate. The Canada-US negotiations were front-page news in Canada from beginning to end but virtually unknown in the United States. As a result, the attention given to the issue by bureaucrats and politicians in the two countries was asymmetrical, a fact of little consequence in Washington but of great moment in Ottawa. From a Canadian point of view, the US side devoted inadequate resources to the negotiations, was often unprepared for

---

cessful experience of the past five years has paved the way for the relatively quick and easy negotiation of a broader bilateral accord.

14 See Peter Morici, "Regionalism in the International Trading System and Mexico-U.S. Trade Relations," paper prepared for the International Forum: Mexico's Trade Options in the Changing International Economy, Universidad Tecnologica de Mexico, Mexico City, June 11-15, 1990, p. 13.

negotiating sessions, did not always think positions through, was too frequently more concerned about setting global precedents than examining the merits of particular issues and was continuously looking over its shoulder at what Congress might think. In short, the US was more enthusiastic about the idea of an agreement than it was prepared to follow through with the necessary resources and commitment to detail.

There is no simple answer to dealing with the United States. Political commitment by the President is simply not enough. Effort must also be devoted to cultivating enthusiasm and support further down among other political and even bureaucratic players.[15] Foreigners too easily overestimate the power of the President in the American scheme of things. To ensure broader support, it is up to foreign governments to demonstrate why the negotiations are in the interest of the United States and develop a strong domestic American constituency prepared to lobby for the agreement. Failure to cultivate such support is likely to lead to failed or unsatisfactory negotiations. Finally, in order to concentrate the American mind, the negotiations need a firm and unalterable deadline. Without such a deadline, the necessary resources and political will to drive the negotiations to an acceptable conclusion will never materialize.

Excessive preoccupation with congressional opinion has become an irritant in all negotiations with the United States and reflects the extent to which the American form of government has become dominated by special interests. It means that foreign governments must devote resources not only to negotiating with the Administration but also to developing support in Congress. Counting on the Administration to carry this task is likely to lead to frustration and disappointment. It also means that negotiations can only be pursued under the authority of the so-called fast-track procedures. Negotiating either a treaty – requiring ratification by two-thirds of the Senate – or an executive agreement – which can be undermined by Congress through its legislative powers – is not recom-

---

[15] The US political decision-making process virtually guarantees imprecision and frequent changes in direction. In Canada, while there are many actors and various levels of influence, in the final analysis federal policy emerges from one source: Cabinet. A role for the provinces in the trade policy-making process is relatively new and its final shape remains to be determined. In the United States, federal policy emerges from a highly brokered political market involving the Administration, Congress, and various special interest groups. Successful policy-making requires coalitions, many of which are forged out of what appear to be unrelated interests. See David Leyton-Brown, "The Domestic Policy-Making Process in the United States" and Allan E. Gotlieb, "The Canada-United States Relationship," in D. H. Flaherty and W. R. McKercher, *Southern Exposure: Canadian Perspectives on the United States* (Toronto: McGraw-Hill Ryerson, 1986).

mended. The fast-track procedure[16] requires continuous congressional liaison but in the end limits Congress to a simple majority yes or no vote on the implementing legislation.

Given the anxiety in most smaller countries about negotiating with a global power, especially a neighbour, it is essential that the drive and desire for an agreement originate in the smaller country. But the need to develop a US constituency and cultivate Congress will give the mistaken impression that the smaller country is desperate for an agreement and will sign almost anything. There is, therefore, need for an adroit balancing act between inspiration and leadership to animate the negotiations and an ability to remain detached about the final result.

Such an adroit balancing act is made more difficult by the need to manage the domestic debate which, given the imbalance in power and interest, will be all-consuming at home while hardly raising a whisper in the United States. The best laid efforts of the Mexican government to manage the domestic debate will be frustrated by callous and cavalier actions in Washington, where the myopia of a great power will sometimes ensure grievous inattention to the political delicacy of some issues in Mexico. As a result, it will be all too easy for opponents of the negotiations to set the agenda. One way to deal with this kind of frustration is to avoid raising expectations too high while maintaining debate at a general level until such time as there is something specific to talk about.

---

16 Under the US constitution, Congress has exclusive power to make trade policy but for practical purposes has since 1934 delegated its negotiating authority to the President subject to congressional oversight and approval. The current "fast-track" negotiating procedures were introduced in 1974 in advance of the Tokyo Round and have been subsequently amended and extended to June 1, 1991. For bilateral negotiations, the procedures are triggered by a request from the proposed partner, which Mexico has now satisfied. As a result, the President must formally notify Congress (the House Ways and Means Committee and the Senate Finance Committee) of his intent to enter into negotiations, a notification which Congress can either ignore or block if it acts within ninety days. Given the fast-approaching deadline of June 1, 1991, the President may submit to Congress no later than March 1, 1991 a request, with reasons, for extension of the fast-track procedure to June 1, 1993. The request would be considered by the same committees and could involve public hearings which would allow Congress to test further the political dimension of any Mexican negotiations. The fact that implementing legislation for the Uruguay Round may be tabled during the same time frame, assuming the round concludes as scheduled at the end of this year, will complicate management of this issue somewhat and has made the Administration reluctant to go to Congress too early or too often. The preferred route is to go to Congress early in 1991 with a package that includes Uruguay Round implementing legislation, notification of intent to negotiate with Mexico (and Canada, if Canada so requests) and extension of the deadline for these negotiations to June 1, 1993.

Mexico's political leaders appear to have these lessons in mind. They have approached the issue cautiously. They have devoted considerable energy to developing a broad domestic constituency favouring negotiations. For many months they were prepared to let others carry the issue until such time as they felt Mexico was ready.[17] Domestic economic reforms are working and not exacting an impossible cost in adjustment. The basis for negotiations in Mexico, therefore, appears to be strong. Equal attention, however, will now have to be devoted not only to the painstaking detail of developing precise negotiating positions, but also to cultivating strong and enduring US support for those positions.

The addition of Canada to the negotiations will be a complicating factor and some US officials have already expressed some qualms about Canadian participation. Canada will bring its own agenda and priorities. Some of these will be directed at the United States; some, at Mexico. On the whole, however, Canadian participation should be of net benefit to the negotiating process. Canadian experience should be a stabilizing influence. More importantly, because Canadian interests are less directly involved and Canada shares some Mexican objectives and some American attitudes and experiences, Canadian negotiators should prove helpful in solving some of the more intransigent issues.

The addition of Canada to the US-Mexico negotiating table would make the negotiation of a trilateral agreement from scratch a less than attractive proposition. While the United States might reluctantly agree to negotiate an agreement with Mexico that starts with a clean sheet of paper, it is unlikely to want to do so once Canada is involved. Canadian involvement would reinforce the natural US tendency to avoid unnecessary duplication and creativity. The division of powers in the United States has always led to one basic tenet in US trade positions: the best agreements are those that require a minimum of legislative change. During the Canada-US bilateral negotiations the US side showed an almost pathological attachment to the letter of the GATT not because US negotiators did not think it could be improved and clarified but because any change in the "familiar" lan-

---

17 As late as March 1990, the official public stance in Mexico was that an FTA with the United States was neither desired nor contemplated. David Crane, the business editor of the *Toronto Star,* after interviewing a range of Mexican officials, including the President, confidently told his readers on March 10, 1990 that a US-Mexico agreement let alone a trilateral deal was highly unlikely. Foreign Secretary Solana told *Maclean's* in March that Mexico was not interested in a free-trade agreement with the United States (*Maclean's,* March 26, 1990, p. 44). Mexican officials changed their tune and provided background briefings on why Mexico wanted a full-fledged agreement once speculation in Washington had showed a more receptive US government than was thought possible. A March 27, 1990 story in the *Wall Street Journal* detailing the degree of preparation underway in the two capitals fuelled this speculation. A strong resolution from the Mexican Senate in April backing a free-trade pact further helped to give these officials confidence.

guage of GATT would make the task of implementing the agreement in domestic law that much more difficult.

Negotiating a North American free-trade agreement will entail hard work. Canada established a team of more than fifty professionals, backed up by another fifty support personnel, access to the resources of many federal and provincial government departments and the help of the private sector. They were considered to be necessary not only to pursue the negotiations and develop the critical analytical base, but also to help manage the political agenda, maintain good relations with the provinces and ensure the continuing support of the private sector. To achieve its objectives, Mexico will have to be prepared to dedicate similar resources and energy to the process.

When and How

Events moved swiftly during the first half of 1990. Academic speculation and general analysis have now been replaced by decisions and action on specific issues. Mexican President Salinas' visit to Washington June 9-11 has set the stage for the preparatory phase. The declaration issued by the two Presidents echoed the Quebec Declaration issued by Prime Minister Mulroney and President Reagan in March of 1985 which set the stage for the Canada-US negotiations. The Mexicans placed great value on such a declaration, hoping that it would have the necessary catalytic effect on investor confidence to maintain the momentum of Mexico's modernization. But more importantly, it has maintained momentum toward the more fundamental step of either a bilateral accord or a trilateral North American agreement.

The June declaration is meant to set the stage for President Bush's visit to Mexico in December. The pace is being set by Mexico with the US President and his advisors prepared to follow that lead. Their advisors further down the ladder, more concerned about detail than grand strategy, would like to slow down the pace. They are signalling that the Administration is reluctant to take the issue to Congress too early. Sentiments are very similar to those Canada experienced five years ago, coloured by a whole host of extraneous issues. While senior politicians in Washington are not overly worried about Congress, their professional strategists are convinced that by waiting until early 1991 they can combine seeking authority for a Mexico negotiation with implementing legislation for the results of the Uruguay Round along with a general extension of the Administration's negotiating authority. They believe that seeking authority for Mexico and an extension in negotiating authority before then would create confusion and take pressure off the need to conclude the Uruguay Round this year.

Worries about the Mexican negotiations complicating the final stages of the Uruguay Round reflect the anxieties of the orthodox multilateralists in USTR. They have a heightened sense of the importance of the Uruguay Round to Congress and to US business and a natural disdain for bilateral or regional adventures. They are unwilling to accept that the negotiation of a North American accord may well capture congressional imagination more effectively than the numbing tedium of GATT negotiations.

Whatever the preferences of the trade policy professionals, events are moving inexorably toward decisions that will not respect such sensitivities about the timetable. The Mexicans are governed by their own imperatives and are unlikely to be swayed by the problems raised by cautious US bureaucrats. Work commissioned by the US-Mexico Business Committee and the US Business Roundtable as well as the April report of the US International Trade Commission have already focussed public debate in the United States on the issue. US and Mexican Congressional elections in 1990 and 1991 respectively, will further raise the profile of the issue as organized labour and other opponents in each country raise their concerns. The AFL-CIO is already on record as opposing an agreement on the grounds that "a free-trade agreement will only encourage greater capital outflow from the United States and bring about a further increase in imports from Mexico, further harming the United States industrial base."[18] Manufacturers in import-sensitive industries are equally unreserved in their opposition. "A free-trade agreement would worsen our already serious import problem and displace U.S. textile and apparel workers," claims Edward Schrum of the American Textile Manufacturers Institute.[19] In short, the issue is on the agenda.

The USTR strategists have not yet determined whether and how to involve Canada. While they accept that the White House and State Department are not averse to making it a three-way negotiation for broad geopolitical reasons, they would prefer to make it a two-way negotiation and not add the complication of Canadian participation. They believe that Canadian involvement holds considerable scope for mischief and eventual grief for American negotiators, given the similarity in objectives of Canada and Mexico. For this reason they are reluctant to seek congressional authority for a three-way negotiation. As usual, USTR caution and skepticism about negotiating with Mexico disappeared once the President, Secretary Baker and their immediate advisors responded with enthusiasm to Mexican overtures. Objections to Canadian participation will similarly disappear in the face of Canadian insistence that a negotiation with Mexico touches vital Canadian interests.

---

18 Quoted in *The New York Times*, June 11, 1990.
19 Quoted in *The Ottawa Citizen*, April 7, 1990.

There is no single congressional view on the merits of either a bilateral US-Mexico accord or a tripartite arrangement. Congress rarely has a monolithic view on anything, made up as it is of a collection of influence-seeking regional and local politicians. The political arithmetic will involve an assessment of how badly the Administration wants an agreement and how prepared it is to make concessions that are important to Congress. It will be heavily influenced by the reaction of American industry and labour. The near-miss on giving the President authority to negotiate an agreement with Canada in 1986 (based on issues totally unrelated to those negotiations) was followed two years later by an overwhelmingly positive vote implementing the agreement because opposition interests were unable to convince a sufficient number of Congressmen and Senators that their interests outweighed those espoused by proponents of the agreement.[20]

In the case of Mexico, opposition will come largely from organized labour and the weaker sectors of the American economy. These represent a declining political force. Organized labour now represents only a small fraction of US workers and the declining sectors no longer control the necessary number of votes in Congress. The textile lobby, for example, can now only count on symbolic votes in Congress, i.e., for legislation that is unlikely to become law. The computer and related industries now employ more people than steel and related industries; IBM is a much more influential voice on the Hill than US Steel. An agreement that promises to tackle investment, services and intellectual property issues in return for more open access for Mexican goods will be enthusiastically supported by the industries of the future. If it provides appropriate phasing and safeguards for the industries of the present, it will also be welcomed by Congress. Organized labour, most concerned about the industries of the past, will only be able to mount a credible case if it is able to marshall the concern of service worker unions by demonstrating that the agreement will undercut their

---

[20] While Canada formally requested negotiations on October 1, 1985, notice was only sent to Congress on December 10, 1985 and was received without fanfare by the two committee chairmen just before the Christmas recess. Informal consultations in January and February suggested that the two committees would be content to let the necessary ninety days elapse without comment and thus allow negotiations to proceed. This was what happened in the House Ways and Means Committee where Congressman Sam Gibbons, chairman of the trade subcommittee, indicated he was a strong supporter of the negotiations and saw no reason to muddy the waters with hearings and a vote before negotiations could even begin. In the Senate, however, strong displeasure with Administration management of trade policy led to an unexpected cliff-hanger tied vote not to disapprove the negotiations. The committee appeared initially inclined to disapprove the request by a substantial margin and the President had to use all of his powers of persuasion to achieve the close vote. Approval to proceed finally came on April 23, 1986 but not before setting strong alarm bells ringing in Canada about the capacity of Administration officials to manage all aspects of the negotiations.

interests. This is what makes the migrant worker issue potentially one of the most difficult on the agenda.

Congress will not care whether such an agreement is with Mexico alone or involves Canada as well. Few congressmen have strong views on the form international agreements take. Again, the views of American business will be critical and American business until now has been cautiously supportive. The US Business Roundtable, representing large transnational corporations, has come out strongly in favour but William T. Archey, of the more broadly representative Chamber of Commerce, warns "It will be much harder to get the same coalition [as supported the Canada-US negotiations] for Mexico. The cost to companies of being out front will be greater."[21]

As with Canada, the cause of a Mexican agreement will have important champions in Congress, without whom the issue will not proceed far. Such champions are to be found in the congressional delegations from the southwest and should eventually include Senator Loyd Bentsen, the powerful chairman of the Senate Finance Committee. Wrote one such champion a few years ago:

Despite recent improvements, congressional thinking about Mexico continues to be guided mostly by parochial concerns. This is not unusual for a body preoccupied with domestic matters, but it is unfortunate for the health of the relationship between our two nations, which depends on an international world outlook. Most often this situation comes not as a deliberate neglect of Mexico's problems, but rather as a lack of awareness and understanding of the growing importance of Mexico in our lives. Our world is too closely interconnected to allow the luxury of ad hoc policy. It is imperative for our relations with Mexico that we develop a cogent economic and political policy.[22]

Now that the Administration has articulated its preliminary views publicly, in response to Mexican preferences, the congressional debate will begin to heat up with highly emotional explorations of every aspect of the issue by individual members of Congress responding to the concerns of constituents and lobbyists. In the end these will make very little difference although they will lend an air of crisis to the negotiations and make them interesting. These will loop back into Canada and Mexico and add to the difficulty of managing the domestic debate in both countries. In the final analysis, outbursts by individual Congressmen and Senators will count for very little and should be treated accordingly.

---

[21] Quoted by Bruce Stokes, "Trade Talks with Mexico Face Hurdles," in *National Journal*, June 16, 1990, p. 1487.

[22] Congressman Jim Kolbe, in a foreword to Sidney Weintraub, *Mexican Trade Policy and the North American Community* (Washington: Center for Strategic and International Studies, 1988), p. viii.

However these problems are resolved in the byzantine world of Washington decision-making, Canada should make up its mind early about what it wants to do and how it wants to use its influence to make sure its interests are factored into any decisions. Trying to catch up after the basic decisions have been made will be much more difficult and costly. Once negotiations are engaged, both sides will have a vital stake in ensuring that the Mexican government can claim success at the end of the day; neither side, therefore, should be expected to take much account of the concerns of a non-participating Canada.

♦♦♦♦♦

6

What Would A Tripartite Agreement Involve?

Should Canada decide that it must participate in the negotiation of a North American free-trade agreement and should the necessary procedural hurdles in all three capitals be cleared, what would be involved in the negotiations? Once Canada decides to participate, the negotiations would for all intents and purposes amount to the trilateralization of the existing FTA. While there are various other ways in which a tripartite arrangement could be achieved, an analysis of the issues involved in trilateralizing the FTA should indicate what most of the difficult issues are and what negotiating challenges have to be met.

Conventional wisdom maintains that the Canada-US FTA is an extremely complex document, the product of intense and difficult negotiations. There is some truth to this assertion but it is a truth that can be easily exaggerated. In point of fact, the FTA is based on more than fifty years of experience in negotiating international trade treaties. Many of the chapters in the agreement follow well trodden paths. Various articles relating to trade in goods, for example, are taken directly from the GATT or provide a particular interpretation of GATT rules. Those that break new ground do so cautiously. The changes in domestic law and practice required by the rights and obligations in the agreement are incremental, i.e., established laws and practices, conforming to the requirements of GATT and other trade treaties, needed incremental adjustments to bring them into conformity with the new, more stringent requirements. Agreement was not reached on the most difficult issues, such as subsidies and countervailing duties, antidumping duties, procurement preferences, supply management, and the protection of intellectual property; it is these issues which would have required more extensive legislative changes.

From this perspective, the task of extending the FTA to Mexico looks less formidable than would at first appear to be the case. For both Canada and the United States, the trade policy arithmetic will be whether the inclusion of Mexico will be of net benefit, i.e., whether the increased competition from low-cost Mexican manufactures will be more than offset by increased and more secure access to the Mexican market for Canadian and US goods, services and investment. Both governments, as well as directly affected interest groups, will need to be convinced that the inclusion of Mexico in the agreement will maintain the agreement's status as a trade-creating rather than trade-diverting agreement.

This kind of arithmetic would have been virtually impossible prior to Mexico's reform of its trade regime in 1985 and its accession to GATT the following year. The combined effect of these two decisions has made the Mexican trade regime sufficiently similar to those of Canada and the United States to allow an assessment of the extent to which it would need to be further adjusted to meet the obligations similar to those in the FTA, or the extent to which Canada and the United States would have to tolerate deviations from those obligations.

Negotiating difficulties will arise less from trade and economic concerns and more from subtle psychological and political perceptions. In Canada and the United States, there will be fears about the deleterious effects of low-cost Mexican labour and about the ability of an economy at a much lower stage of development to compete fairly with two industrialized economies. Mexicans will worry about the threat of enhanced American influence and dominance. An economic analysis based on classic international trade theory should demonstrate the short-term adjustment costs and long-term economic benefits flowing from a more integrated North American economy. But such an analysis cannot deal adequately with deep-seated fears and long-held prejudices. In crafting a basis for Mexican accession, therefore, the three governments will have to be sensitive to these non-economic concerns without letting them overwhelm their trade policy judgments.

Neither Canada nor the United States is likely to be prepared to make major adjustments in the text of the FTA, although there are some areas which could benefit from the wisdom of several years' experience. Having laboured two years to negotiate the agreement, they will not regard the renegotiation of the text as an attractive option. Negotiating a protocol of accession is perhaps the most attractive scenario for Canada and the United States but may not be adequate in addressing Mexican concerns. We need not, however, let the mechanics of Mexican accession to the FTA or of some other form of tripartite cooperation stand in the way of the analysis, which is valid whichever method is chosen.

A major issue will be whether there is a case for asymmetry, e.g., a longer phase-in of obligations for Mexico than for Canada and the United States. In the case of the US-Israel FTA, the United States was prepared to phase in various provisions of the agreement on a differential basis recognizing Israel's status as a developing country.[1] Mexico may well press for similar treatment and will be able to mount a good political case. Not only will it be able to plead its case as a developing country, but it will also be in a good position to argue that its unilateral reforms should be recognized and compensated through differential treatment. Mexico's accession to the GATT stressed its status as a developing country and its ability, under the terms of article XVIII, part IV and the 1979 Decision on Safeguard Action for Development Purposes, to maintain measures otherwise inconsistent with the GATT. While Mexico's unilateral reform program has gone well beyond the commitments it made upon acceding to the GATT in 1986, these commitments are not binding and Mexico might well resist making all of them contractual.

Any efforts by Mexico to seek permanent differential treatment for more than a few specific instances should be treated as a non-starter. In the unlikely event that domestic pressures dispose Mexico to seek such treatment, a North American FTA is not the right vehicle to underwrite further economic reform. The GATT provides for such treatment and Mexico would have to be encouraged to limit its obligations to those contained in GATT. A permanent differential regime would undermine the desired economic effects of a trilateral accord and eventually erode support for it in Canada and the United States.

The major challenge will thus be to Mexico whose trade and investment regime has long been out of step with international practice. While the unilateral reform has already forced a major realignment in its trade laws and practices, it still has a way to go. As noted above, as a developing country there are various aspects of GATT with which it did not need to conform. Additionally, it is able to justify various practices under the terms of its protocol of accession. Entering into

---

1 For a discussion of the US-Israel Agreement, see Dennis James Jr., "The Agreement on Establishment of a Free Trade Area between the Government of the United States of America and the Government of Israel: Background and Analysis," in Maureen Irish and Emily F. Carasco, eds., *The Legal Framework for Canada-United States Trade* (Toronto: Carswell, 1987), pp. 121-130.

a trilateral free-trade arrangement, therefore, would require it to build upon these adjustments and go much further in bringing its regime into line with those of Canada and the United States.

The following pages use the FTA as a prism through which to examine the trade regimes of the three countries and the extent to which they would have to be adjusted in order to reach a trilateral accord. They seek to isolate those issues that would appear to be the most difficult for Canada, the United States or Mexico.

The Canada-US FTA: An Overview [2]

The Free-Trade Agreement required Canada and the United States to eliminate the tariff and remove a wide variety of other import barriers and domestic practices or bring them under codes of conduct based on the principle of national treatment. The trade liberalizing elements of the agreement are being phased in over a period of up to ten years to provide industry with the time to adjust to more competitive conditions. The agreement is thus exposing Canadian and American farmers, producers, manufacturers and service providers to stiffer competition but within a predictable framework of rules that assure them greater and more secure access to a combined and integrated market. The reward for accepting more intense competition is the opportunity of exploiting that much larger market.[3]

The preamble and first chapter set out the basic objectives of the two governments and provide the philosophical framework within which the whole agree-

---

[2] This section is based on excerpts from an earlier article, "The Future on the Table: The Continuing Negotiating Agenda under the Canada-United States Free Trade Agreement," in Richard G. Dearden, Michael M. Hart and Debra P. Steger, eds., *Living with Free Trade: Canada, the Free Trade Agreement and the GATT* (Halifax and Ottawa: The Institute for Research on Public Policy and The Centre for Trade Policy and Law, 1990), pp. 67-131.

[3] The FTA and the debate preceding and during the negotiations have generated a lively and growing literature. Among commentaries on the Agreement and its implications, see Murray G. Smith and Frank Stone, eds., *Assessing the Canada-U.S. Free Trade Agreement* (Halifax: The Institute for Research on Public Policy, 1987); Jeffrey J. Schott and Murray G. Smith, eds., *The Canada-United States Free Trade Agreement: The Global Impact* (Ottawa and Washington: Institute for Research on Public Policy and Institute for International Economics, 1988); William Diebold, Jr., ed., *Bilateralism, Multilateralism and Canada in US Trade Policy* (New York: Council on Foreign Relations, 1988); Richard G. Lipsey and Robert C. York, *Evaluating the Free Trade Deal: A Guided Tour through the Canada-U.S. Agreement* (Toronto: C. D. Howe Institute, 1988); Donald M. McRae and Debra P. Steger, eds., *Understanding the Free Trade Agreement* (Halifax: Institute for Research on Public Policy, 1988); and Jon R. Johnson and Joel S. Schachter, *The Free Trade Agreement: A Comprehensive Guide* (Toronto: Canada Law Book, 1988).

ment must be viewed. The heart of the agreement can be found in chapters 3 to 13. These establish a sound but conventional free-trade agreement. They provide a sensible set of rules fully consistent with GATT article XXIV. The link to GATT cannot be overemphasized. Many of the clauses of the agreement are drawn directly out of the GATT or provide agreed interpretations of GATT provisions.[4] In effect, the FTA takes a set of good rules and makes them better. Where either side was not prepared to go as far as the other, provision was made to continue negotiations, but within a new and more secure framework.[5]

Chapters 14 to 17 make a cautious start on the so-called new issues of services, business travel, investment and financial services. They recognize that international commerce is more than a matter of shipping goods to one another. The two governments decided to freeze the status quo and to promise that any future laws and regulations would be based on the premise that Canada and the United States will treat each other's service providers, investors and business travellers as they treat their own.

Chapters 18 and 19 achieve a Canadian quest of long standing – a contractual, institutional basis for managing the trade and economic relationship. Chapter 18 takes well-established GATT practice, commits it to a clear body of rules and procedures, and applies these to the rights and obligations of the agreement as a whole – to the enhanced and improved GATT-like rules dealing with trade in goods as well as the new rules dealing with services, investment and business travel. For the first time, there is a clear mechanism that places Canada and the United States on an equal, one-on-one footing. The agreement as a whole provides the rules; chapter 18 furnishes a neutral referee to enforce those rules. In ef-

---

4 For example: Article 104 provides a general affirmation of GATT rights and obligations, as well as any other pre-existing rights and obligations under other agreements, such as the Autopact; Articles 407 and 409 and 902 and 904 clarify existing GATT rights and obligations under GATT Articles I, II, XI, XIII and XX with respect to import and export restrictions and prohibitions; Article 501 incorporates Article III of the GATT respecting national treatment rights and obligations; Article 602 affirms rights and obligations under the GATT *Agreement on Technical Barriers*; Article 710 affirms GATT rights with respect to supply management measures under article XI; Article 1201 incorporates the exceptions clauses of GATT Article XX; Chapter 13 builds on the GATT *Agreement on Government Procurement*; Article 1801 affirms the right of the two parties to solve disputes arising under either the GATT or the FTA in either forum, for example in regard to FTA Article 501/GATT Article III; Article 2010 is a modernized version of GATT Article XVII regarding state-trading practices; and Article 2011 incorporates parts of GATT Article XXIII.

5 Growing pains in the implementation and administration of the agreement are regularly chronicled in two newsletters devoted to Canada-US trade relations: *The Free Trade Observer* published by Carswell and *The Free Trade Reporter* published by *The Globe and Mail* and *American Banker Newsletter*.

fect these chapters provide a contractual basis for the special relationship which Canadians have long assumed existed between Canada and the United States. By placing that relationship on a contractual footing, the two countries have underscored the extent to which trade relations have shifted from being largely diplomatic to being progressively more legalistic.

Chapter 19 deals with the thorny issue of trade remedies. Here the United States recognizes for the first time that disputes arising out of the application of trade remedy laws are not a matter for the application of domestic law and unilateral decisions alone, but should also be subject to bilateral dispute settlement. The chapter provides an important beginning. While both countries will continue to rely on their respective trade remedy laws, they have agreed to replace judicial review of domestic decisions by bilateral review, to subject amendments of their laws to bilateral challenge and to continue negotiations toward a replacement regime.

The provisions of the agreement as a whole offer a significant improvement in the security and stability of Canadian access to the United States market. For example:

- changes in antidumping and countervailing duty laws have to name Canada specifically and are subject to a declaratory judgment as to their conformity with US GATT obligations and the object and purpose of the agreement;
- binding dispute settlement will substantially inhibit political fixes from distorting the application of antidumping and countervailing duties and should impede the launch and acceptance of frivolous suits;
- escape clause action against Canadian exports can only be taken where these exports alone are the cause of serious injury to US industry or where such exports are above ten percent of total US imports of the product in question and undermine the effectiveness of global US restrictions;
- national treatment in services will prevent new trade restrictive action against Canadian exports in the service sectors designated in the agreement; and
- national treatment in investment will prevent the addition of new discriminatory barriers to Canadian investors and assure them of equitable treatment once established.

Finally, the agreement provides a framework for the negotiations of the future. At least ten articles throughout the agreement anticipate continued negotiations. The most important of these relate to subsidies, anticompetitive pricing practices, intellectual property and government procurement.

Canadian and US interest in a bilateral agreement, while not identical, proved compatible and negotiable. The result is a workmanlike agreement that satisfies many of the basic objectives of both Canadians and Americans, as well as establishing a framework for further improving the agreement. Mexican interests and objectives are not fundamentally different from those of Canada and the United States. Mexico is similarly seeking secure access to a large enough market to further underwrite domestic economic reform. It has made sufficient progress unilaterally to be convinced that it is on the right track and that the short-term political costs are worth the long-term economic benefits. What needs to be determined now is whether these broad objectives can be translated into specific rights and obligations that fit within a framework of rights and obligations similar to those contained in the FTA.

A Chapter-by-Chapter Analysis of the FTA

Preamble and Chapter One: Objectives

In most agreements, the preamble and statement of objectives do little more than provide the political framework within which the rest of the agreement must be considered. In the Canada-US FTA, however, chapter nineteen provides that any changes in domestic antidumping and countervailing duty laws are subject to challenge on the basis of the "object and purpose" of the agreement, giving the preamble and chapter added significance. Additionally, chapter one includes a stronger version of the GATT federal-state clause and provisions on the order of precedence of this agreement as compared to other bilateral and multilateral agreements.

A close examination of the contents of the preamble and chapter one discloses no major difficulty that might arise if these rights and obligations were extended to Mexico. While there might be need for one or two additional preambular phrases to satisfy Mexican political imperatives, there are none there now that should trouble any of the three governments if they were adjusted to include Mexico.

Article 101, which contains a bold assertion of GATT consistency, might well have been tested by the time any trilateral negotiations are joined. A GATT Working Party is now seized of the Canada-US FTA and should decide by the end of 1990 whether the FTA complies with the requirements of GATT. In keeping with past GATT practice, the Working Party is likely to prepare an inconclusive report, which the parties to an FTA have traditionally taken to mean that their agreement meets the requirements of GATT.[6]

Articles 102-105 are all straightforward and should be adaptable to Mexican accession without any significant difficulty. Article 102, objectives, establishes the broad parameters of the agreement and is unexceptional. While Mexico has a federal state structure similar to those of Canada and the United States, the division of powers is such that it is unlikely to face the kind of challenges to federal authority that can be launched in Canada. Article 103 (extent of obligations), therefore, should present no challenge to Mexico. Article 104 (affirmation and precedence) is largely of a technical nature and non-controversial and article 105 (national treatment) establishes no specific rights or obligations other than those spelled out in more detail in the rest of the agreement.

Chapter Two: Definitions

The general definitions chapter of the agreement would need some adjustment to incorporate Mexican practice. The idea of defining terms precisely as they are used in the agreement as a whole, and in each chapter as they are used within that chapter, an innovation in this international trade agreement borrowed from domestic legal practice, has proven prudent. Negotiating a trilateral accord to include Mexico might well provide scope to strengthen this provision. Given the pressure of time that attended the legal drafting of the agreement, it was not possible to isolate all those words that required definition. Expanding the list of defined terms, however, is largely a technical task of legal drafting and should not excite much controversy nor have any substantive impact on existing rights and obligations.

Chapter Three: Rules of Origin

In many ways, chapter three, which establishes the rules of origin for the Agreement, may be the most difficult and the most important chapter that will have to be tackled in negotiating Mexican accession. In effect, the chapter contains hundreds if not thousands of product-specific rules of origin. While Article 301 sets out the general rule and Article 304 the all-important definitions, the real rules are contained in Annex 301.2 which sets out how the general rules will be applied on a product-specific basis. It requires that individual producers know precisely how the rules apply to the products that they wish to trade on a duty-

---

6   The requirements of Article XXIV and the nature of GATT's consideration of free-trade
      agreements are discussed in Michael Hart, "GATT Article XXIV and the Canada-United
      States Trade Negotiations," in *Review of International Business Law*, Vol. 1, No. 3 (December,
      1987), pp. 317-355.

free basis and it means that the rules can be readily adjusted to meet specific and changing circumstances. The advantage of what appears at first to be a highly complex system is that, once the basic rule and its application are understood by individual manufacturers, it becomes a predictable and unchanging rule. It will not, for example, be subjected to the vagaries of changing interpretation as has been the case for the more widely applied US substantial transformation rule. In effect, the FTA specifies what substantial transformation means in every instance and limits the application of a 50 per cent value added rule to the situations where it makes economic sense or was politically necessary.

The rules of origin are based on the new Harmonized System (HS) of tariff classification. The HS is based on the long established and widely used Brussels Tariff Nomenclature and its successor, the Customs Cooperation Council Tariff Nomenclature, but its concepts are new to Canada and the United States. Canada introduced the HS in 1988 and the United States in 1989. Inevitably, therefore, the two customs administrations are experiencing some growing pains in applying the new system and these are influencing their experience with the application of the rules of origin. Mexico uses the HS tariff nomenclature and used the Brussels and CCC systems before that. Unlike the original Canada-US negotiations, therefore, all three parties would now be proceeding on the basis of a common tariff nomenclature and system.

Negotiating a tripartite deal will involve a detailed assessment, on a product-by-product basis, of the impact of extending the rules to include products wholly or partially manufactured in Mexico. This will require detailed consultations and will excite some concerns. Those companies in Canada, for example, which expressed anxiety about US goods incorporating products benefitting from the Mexican Maquiladora program will be even more anxious if such goods qualify for duty-free treatment. Similarly, there will be companies concerned that Mexico will become a conduit for Japanese, Brazilian or other third-country goods. As a result, it can be expected that there will be manufacturers in Canada and the United States who will seek more stringent rules. For example, there will be requests to extend the fifty percent FTA content provision to more products or to require chapter to chapter transformation rather than heading to heading transformation. The rules as they now stand reflect an assessment of Canadian and US industrial structures. The addition of Mexico will change that assessment and require detailed adjustment.

Given the increasingly integrated structure of industry in North America and the rationalization that is taking place to take advantage of global markets, it is not realistic to consider a permanent separate set of rules of origin for Mexico, as might be suggested by some manufacturers worried about competing with

Mexico. In effect, demands for separate or tougher rules amount to demands to use the rules of origin to deny the benefits of tariff elimination. They indicate the extent to which in a free-trade negotiation protectionist concerns can be met through artful drafting of the rules of origin rather than through tariff exemption.

The eventual goal should be a single rule of origin based on North American content, i.e., products wholly of Canadian, US and Mexican origin in any combination always qualify while products that incorporate some non-North American content qualify depending on the degree of transformation and/or value added in <u>any</u> of the three countries. There may be need, however, for a transitional rule. From a Canadian perspective, such a rule would treat goods of Mexican or mixed US-Mexican origin differently from goods that meet the current FTA rules. Such a rule would recognize the fact that Canada and the United States maintain different tariffs to third countries and would thus be eliminating a different tariff structure. The challenge would be to construct a transitional rule that would not become a major disincentive to firms wishing to take advantage of improved access to the integrated market.

The rules for trade in textiles and clothing may be even more controversial in the US-Mexico and Canada-Mexico context than they were in the Canada-US negotiations. Long used to high levels of protection, these two industries have learned to press their case with great vigour in the two capitals. While not as potent as they once were and thus no longer able to block the negotiation of a tripartite arrangement, they remain sufficiently strong to insist that the rules of origin be so structured as to prevent any pass-through potential for inputs from third countries and to demand that the United States and Canada maintain quotas to limit the extent of duty-free trade. Mexico, eager to exploit the advantages of a larger market for an industry where it enjoys a competitive edge, will stoutly resist both punitive rules of origin and tariff-rate quotas.

Even without Mexican accession, we are likely to see some significant lobbying in Canada (and, to a lesser extent, the United States) to adjust the rules of origin to changing business reality. Not all businesses are happy with the rules and some have found them to be a significant barrier to taking advantage of the tariff provisions of the FTA. Some companies have concluded that the cost of meeting the rules of origin exceeds the benefits of duty-free or lower tariff treatment and are continuing to do business under the MFN tariff regime.

The numbing complexity and tedium of rules of origin should not lull government and business analysts into complacency about this chapter. Negotiating a workable and politically acceptable set of rules is critical to the success of any free-trade agreement. Given current criticisms of the rules, it is possible that insufficient attention was paid to this fact by Canadian business and the federal government during the FTA negotiations. The accession of Mexico might well be viewed, therefore, as a convenient opportunity to rectify this situation.[7]

On a related note, efforts in the Uruguay Round to develop uniform rules of origin are unlikely to lead to detailed agreement. Nonetheless, these discussions have clearly identified the need for model rules of origin that can be applied in the various circumstances in which such rules are required. The FTA rules of origin, for example, are limited in their application to determining appropriate tariff treatment. They do not apply to the operation of trade remedy law, government procurement or other border measures. Additionally, there are different rules applied by Canada and the United States to goods of non-FTA origin (e.g., for GSP treatment). In recognition of the difficulties for traders raised by a multiplicity of complex and incompatible rules, GATT and the Customs Cooperation Council have initiated efforts to develop a uniform or model code. While agreement in the Uruguay Round is not likely to go beyond the development of broad principles and a work program leading toward harmonization, these discussions should also help to create a more constructive atmosphere within which to consider the development of rules of origin for a North American free-trade accord.

Chapter Four: Border Measures

If the problems of chapter three can be successfully resolved, the issues raised by chapter four may prove relatively uncomplicated. The issues here can be divided into two groups: those related to the tariff and those arising from other border measures.

The main tariff question is the speed with which the tariff will be eliminated for trade between Canada and Mexico and the United States and Mexico. In the FTA, Canada and the United States agreed to eliminate the tariff on the basis of three formulas: immediate elimination; elimination in five annual steps; and elimination in ten annual steps. The decision where to place individual tariff items followed from intense industry consultations.

A similar approach could be adopted in negotiating Mexican accession. Given the lower cost structure of some Mexican industries, however, there are likely to be many more requests for extended rather than accelerated tariff elimination. At

---

7   For a critical examination of the rules of origin, see N. David Palmeter, "The FTA Rules of Origin: Boon or Boondoggle?," in Richard G. Dearden, Michael M. Hart and Debra P. Steger, eds., *Living with Free Trade: Canada, the Free Trade Agreement and the GATT* (Halifax and Ottawa: The Institute for Research on Public Policy and The Centre for Trade Policy and Law, 1990), pp. 41-48.

the same time Mexico, which has already adjusted to a significant reduction in tariff protection over the last few years, may be reluctant to eliminate the remainder too quickly. A realistic negotiating scenario, therefore, might involve the elimination of most tariffs over a period of ten, twelve or even fifteen years with provision for faster elimination for those industries that believe they are ready.

There is no compelling reason for Canada and the United States to offer a common approach to tariff elimination other than that of business simplicity. As long as the three countries work out a relatively straightforward set of formulas, the individual tariff schedules will then itemize who will eliminate what tariffs at what pace.

Mexico bound its tariff in GATT at 50 percent ad valorem but its maximum applied rate is 20 percent with many tariff positions attracting rates of 5, 10 and 15 percent. The overall incidence of the tariff on a trade-weighted basis is now under 10 percent, comparable to that of Canada and double that of the United States for MFN trade, a drop from close to 30 percent prior to the 1985 unilateral reforms.[8] The major adjustment resulting from tariff elimination, therefore, has already been undertaken and the issue of tariff elimination should not be exaggerated for any of the three countries.

For Canada and the United States, remaining high tariffs affecting imports from Mexico are in labour intensive sectors such as textiles, clothing and footwear where Mexico's labour-cost advantage is such as to be able to jump over high tariffs. Penetration by Mexico of the Canadian market for these products, however, is not very high. While Mexico developed a respectable industry to satisfy domestic demand, any plans to develop an export-oriented industry were frustrated by the imposition of quotas at a relatively low level by the United States and the European Community under the GATT Multifibre Agreement.[9] As a result, these are not export-oriented sectors in Mexico nor those where new investment is taking place. Rather, Mexican manufacturers are concentrating their export activities in other sectors, particularly machinery and transportation equipment, where tariffs are not very high. Additionally, the whole issue of "cheap" Mexican labour should be examined much more critically than has been done heretofore. Wages are lower because the productivity of a largely unskilled

---

[8]   See footnote 11 in chapter three above.

[9]   Because the US and EC in effect cut off the development of an export-oriented industry in Mexico at an early stage, Canada has never needed to negotiate export restraints with Mexico along lines similar to those negotiated with East Asian suppliers of low-cost textiles and clothing. Eighty percent of the value of Mexican textile and clothing exports to the United States are covered by quotas. See Sidney Weintraub, *A Marriage of Convenience: Relations Between Mexico and the United States* (New York: Oxford University Press, 1990), p. 80.

or semi-skilled labour force remains low. As productivity improves, so will labour costs. Furthermore, labour is only one cost component and, in many industries, a component of decreasing importance.

Most Mexican products benefit from preferential tariff treatment in Canada and, to a lesser extent, the United States, narrowing the amount of remaining tariff protection that would be eliminated by an FTA; 82 percent of Mexico's exports to Canada in 1989 were duty-free, either on an MFN basis or as a result of the GPT. Similarly, a high proportion of Mexico's exports to the United States benefit from duty-free or lower GSP-duty treatment. In short, it is not the tariff that is responsible for the low level of Canada-Mexico trade and the elimination of the tariff alone would not greatly increase two-way trade. Rather, the elimination of the tariff on a three-way basis should encourage greater rationalization throughout North American and thus stimulate greater economic activity in all three countries.

As noted, Mexico uses the Harmonized System of tariff nomenclature, a fact which should greatly facilitate tariff negotiations since all three countries will be operating on the basis of roughly equivalent tariff systems. Mexico is also a party to the GATT Customs Valuation Code, reducing possible controversy about valuation. Since acceding to GATT, Mexico has virtually eliminated its former practice of official prices for customs purposes.

Most of the rest of chapter four reflects some of the peculiarities of Canadian and US customs practice. Much of it involves an affirmation or clarification of GATT rights and obligations. It will need, however, some provisions to reflect Mexican practices as well as a judgment that its provisions can be extended by Canada and the United States to Mexico.

For Canada, this will involve a decision whether it is prepared to make the same concessions to Mexico regarding its duty drawback and remission programs as it did to the United States.

The United States will have to decide whether it is prepared to eliminate its customs user fees for Mexico, a measure it is already under pressure to bring into conformity with GATT, and adjust its program for duty-free zones. Mexico has equivalent practices which would need to be brought into conformity. The fact that the US and Mexico both impose customs' user fees may provide a basis for trading equivalent concessions.

For Mexico, the main issue will involve addressing the remaining vestiges of its old import substitution regime, including its prior import licensing scheme, the extent to which the Maquiladora program will have to be adjusted to bring it into conformity with the obligations in article 404 relating to drawbacks and free-trade zones, export licenses and duties, import and export subsidies, dual exchange rates and customs user fees. While Mexico has made great strides in reforming its trade regime, there remains room for reform. As well, many of the reforms have been implemented on the basis of administrative decrees rather than legislation. An accord would provide the security of legislation. If given enough time to phase in changes with assurance of secure access to the US and Canadian markets, Mexico should be able to make those adjustments.

The obligations in article 406 and its annex are similar to a recent agreement on customs cooperation between Canada and Mexico and similar arrangements between the United States and Mexico and hence present no particular difficulties. While these agreements were largely motivated by efforts to control trade in illicit drugs, they are equally applicable to normal trade.

The obligation in article 407 relating to exports to and imports from third countries that affect trade with either Canada or the United States will create some difficulties because of its security implications. For Canada and the United States, given their long record of cooperation in controlling trade in sensitive products, particularly through COCOM in Paris, the article recognized existing practice. There is no such record of cooperation involving Mexico. While the reduction of East-West tensions has diminished the vigilance with which the US regards trade in high technology and military products, the third-country trade issue will remain a sensitive issue in any tripartite negotiation and will have to be dealt with carefully.

Finally, Mexico will have to consider whether it is prepared to accept the obligation in article 408 prohibiting export taxes and the obligations relating to access to resources in article 409. They build upon but expand GATT obligations and will prove particularly difficult in the context of energy trade and as such are discussed further in the context of the energy chapter. More generally, however, the United States is unlikely to be prepared to make any significant changes in these articles, arguing that in return for open and more secure access to its large market, Mexico should be prepared to commit itself to being a reliable supplier, if not immediately, then within a reasonable period of time. Neither Canada nor the United States should face difficulty extending the obligations of articles 408-409 to Mexico.

Generally speaking, therefore, the provisions of chapter four, while requiring some hard bargaining and tedious technical work, do not appear to raise insuperable obstacles to the negotiation of a tripartite North American free-trade agreement.

Chapter Five: National Treatment

This should not be a controversial chapter. Article 501 amounts to a straightforward incorporation of GATT article III (national treatment) into the FTA. Article 502 extends these obligations to the states and provinces in a recognition of evolving practice and of GATT jurisprudence arising out of GATT article XXIV:12 (the federal state clause).[10] Given Mexico's accession to GATT, there should be no problem for any of the three governments involved. The GATT Working Party examining Mexican accession in 1986 raised no problems relating to article III.

Nevertheless, some careful research will have to be undertaken to catalogue those Mexican practices that are incompatible with GATT article III and justified on the basis of its protocol of accession. The United States, for example, continues to justify discriminatory marking requirements on the basis that its 1933 law requiring marks of origin predates the GATT and is thus exempted under the Protocol of Provisional Application.[11] Any such laws and practices that are so identified for Mexico should be brought into conformity either immediately or eventually or should be specifically exempted.

Since there may be an unknown number of residual discriminatory practices, the United States may be more willing to consider a "saving" clause such as was proposed but rejected during the FTA negotiations. Such a clause would prescribe that all restrictions and discriminatory practices are illegal except as specifically provided in the agreement.

Chapter Six: Technical Standards

This is also not a particularly controversial chapter. Technical regulations for health, safety, sanitary and consumer protection reasons can constitute severe barriers to trade if they are applied in a discriminatory or arbitrary manner, but the right to maintain regulations to protect human, animal and plant life, the environment or for a variety of other purposes is a sovereign issue for each country to decide. The ability to make such decisions is fully protected in both the GATT

---

10 A number of GATT cases involving Canadian provincial policies, particularly liquor board practices, have interpreted the GATT federal state clause more stringently than had traditionally been considered the extent of the obligation, in effect blurring the distinction between GATT article XXIV and FTA article 103.

11 See footnote 22 in chapter three above.

and the FTA. The challenge is to ensure that such rules are not abused and become disguised protectionist trade measures.

In this chapter, Canada and the United States affirm their obligations under the GATT Agreement on Technical Barriers to Trade to avoid the use of standards-related measures as unnecessary obstacles to trade. The Agreement establishes the general principle of national treatment. It requires that the two governments treat goods originating in the other country identically to goods of domestic origin once they have satisfied all customs formalities, including any technical standards requirements. The two governments will also endeavour to make their respective standards-related measures and procedures more compatible and thus reduce the obstacles to trade and the costs of exporting which arise from having to meet different standards. Since many standards-related measures are developed by private organizations in Canada and the United States (such as the Canadian Standards Association or the Underwriters Laboratory), and they have already made much progress in developing compatible standards, all that the two governments can do is encourage these organizations to continue to work toward greater consistency.

The issue, therefore, is whether Mexico is prepared to accelerate the process of bringing its technical standards and standards-setting procedures into greater conformity with those of Canada and the United States. The practical exigencies of modern trade are already proving a powerful inducement to meet this requirement, but there are political concerns, as we saw in Canada, about "harmonizing" to the US standard. Mexico joined the GATT Standards Code in 1988 and is taking steps to bring its standards and standards-setting procedures into conformity with the code. Standardization is one of the principal issues being pursued under the 1989 US-Mexico Understanding Regarding Trade and Investment Talks. Thus, on a bilateral basis, the US has already made a good beginning in acquainting Mexican officials with what is involved in moving toward trade-neutral product standards, testing, packaging, certification and related regulations. Mexican officials are similarly sensitizing US officials to the fact that some US standards are unduly rigorous and may pose an unnecessary non-tariff barrier to trade.

Chapter Seven: Agriculture

Chapter seven marks the first substantially controversial chapter in the agreement, but not so much for Canada as for the United States. Generally, the agriculture discussion will be controversial less because of the rights and obligations in the agreement than because of their absence. While the FTA contains relatively greater obligations in the agricultural sector than other free-trade agreements, they are significantly less onerous than obligations for trade in industrial goods.[12] As it stands, the FTA eliminates all agricultural tariffs and a number of specific non-tariff barriers. Some of the most important barriers to trade in agriculture are not addressed. The various price support mechanisms used in Canada and the United States, such as deficiency payments, import quotas and supply management, are not covered. Provision is made, however, for continued negotiations, both multilaterally and bilaterally. Thus the degree of difficulty in extending this chapter to Mexico depends in part on the extent to which Canada and the United States are prepared to go further bilaterally at the conclusion of the Uruguay Round – which in turn depends on what is achieved in the Round.

It is impossible to predict what will be accomplished in the Uruguay Round on agricultural subsidies. The United States and the EC have long been locked in a battle of nerves as to who will disarm first in the expensive game of subsidizing farm production. While Canada also subsidizes agricultural production, albeit for a different mix of products than does the United States, progress will only come when the EC decides to dismantle the main machinery of its Common Agricultural Policy and the United States retreats from the policies enshrined in the Agricultural Adjustment Act of 1933 and subsequent Farm Bills, both given GATT exemption by a 1955 waiver. Additionally, both engage in competitive export subsidization which has further distorted world agriculture trade and needs desperately to be brought under control. While both governments are convinced that the other's programs are unacceptable, there is reluctance to recognize that real reform has to start at home. Thus the results of the Round may be as much cosmetic as real.

While Mexico may want more open and secure access for its exports of seasonal fruits and vegetables, its agricultural sector remains extremely sensitive. The unilateral program of reforms barely touches the agricultural sector. During the import substitution drive of the 1960s and 1970s, agriculture kept pace with demand from an increasingly urban population, but during the oil boom and crisis, a heavy program of subsidization of basic food led to drops in domestic supply of these commodities and shifts to higher value products, distorting agricultural production. Much of the Mexican economy remains rural, and near-subsistence peasant farming still plays a central role in many states. Some seven percent of Mexican GDP is generated in agriculture, involving about a third of the population on either a part-time or full-time basis.[13]

---

12 The 1960 Treaty of Stockholm establishing the European Free Trade Agreement (EFTA), for example, exempts agriculture altogether, as do the individual free-trade agreements concluded in the early 1970s between individual EFTA members and the European Community.

13 The problems of Mexican agriculture are discussed in Gary D. Thompson and Jimmye S. Hillman, "Agricultural Trade between the United States and Mexico: The Impact of Mexico's

Table 13
Mexican Trade in Agriculture with Canada and the United States
(millions of US dollars)

	1984		1987	
Sector	Canada	USA	Canada	USA
Total Exports	818	18,020	932	20,721
food and live animals	40	1,001	70	668
beverages and tobacco	-	2	-	5
crude agricultural materials	28	1,307	50	1,037
Total Imports	267	11,474	424	14,058
food and live animals	55	1,555	76	2,202
beverages and tobacco	7	105	8	186
crude agricultural materials	6	260	2	607

Source: Adapted from Statistics Canada, *Merchandise Trade: Imports* (Cat. 65203, 1988 and 1989) and US Department of Commerce, *Statistical Abstracts of the United States,* 1986 and 1989.

Although agricultural negotiations between the US and Mexico could be extremely difficult, the impact on Canada's farmers should be modest. The US supplies 85 percent of Mexico's food imports – between $1 and $1.5 billion annually – but during critical marketing periods, Mexican fruits and vegetables worth about $2 billion annually compete with produce from the US South. Canada-Mexico agricultural trade, on the other hand, is generally complementary. Canada buys Mexican-produced fruits and vegetables during the winter months worth about $100 million annually, while Mexico buys Canada's grains, oilseeds and skim milk powder. More than 90 percent of Canada's $150 million agricultural exports enter Mexico free of duty.

Discussion between the United States and Mexico of the provisions of article 702 (special provisions for fresh fruits and vegetables) should prove particularly interesting. Canada should be able to play largely a bystander role here, taking quiet satisfaction in seeing a reversal in US attitudes and concerns.

Articles 704 - 707, providing specific commitments regarding market access for meat, grain and grain products, poultry and eggs, and sugar-containing products reflect the peculiarities of Canadian and US agricultural regulation and could not be directly adapted to Mexico. Rather, in the light of the results of the

Foreign Debt," *American Journal of Agricultural Economics,* vol. 71, no. 5 (December 1989), pp. 1123-1137 and Sara J. Scherr, "Agriculture in an Export Boom Economy: A Comparative Analysis of Policy and Performance in Indonesia, Mexico and Nigeria," *World Development,* vol. 17, no. 4 (April 1989), pp. 543-560.

Uruguay Round, the three countries would either have to negotiate more generic rights and obligations or negotiate specific commitments that take into account the peculiarities of Mexican agriculture. As noted, the latter would be much more difficult for the United States and Mexico while the former would pose a major challenge to all three. Given the historic difficulty of negotiating agricultural trade agreements, specific commitments are more likely and could involve a fair degree of asymmetry.

In the case of phytosanitary regulations (health and safety regulations relating to agricultural commodities), there is a detailed program for consultation laid out in an annex to Article 708. It establishes a contractual framework within which the respective agricultural authorities will work to eliminate unnecessary differences in their health regulations. This work program could ostensibly be extended to include Mexico, but not without some difficulty. Mexican officials consider US agricultural standards to be excessive while US officials are well aware that any lowering of standards or delegation of inspection requirements to Mexico will not be well received by the American (or Canadian) public, either on its merits or on the basis of fears generated by interested parties. Again, bilateral US-Mexico discussions may already be smoothing the path toward more uniform standards but the issue will remain very sensitive.

Chapter Eight: Alcoholic Beverages

Chapter eight addresses a specific irritant in Canada-US relations and as such should excite little controversy in trilateral discussion. The results of the 1987 GATT panel examining European complaints about Canadian liquor board practices as well as bilateral discussions with the Americans and Europeans have significantly reduced the scope of this issue. Nevertheless, there remain issues to be resolved, particularly in the beer sector where the complaint of the G. Heilemann Brewing Company under section 301 has led to a US request for a GATT panel.[14]

Mexico and the United States have already reached a bilateral accord on beer and wine. As part of the 1987 sectoral accords, Mexico agreed to eliminate import quotas and licensing requirements for beer and wine. As a result, the United States has largely achieved its major objectives for this sector in both markets. The US maintains no major restrictions on imports of alcoholic beverages.

---

[14] The petition was formally accepted on June 29, 1990 by the United States Trade Representative setting the stage for a formal inquiry and dispute settlement procedures. See *The Free Trade Observer*, No. 9, June, 1990, pp. 106-107.

Mexico is not a major producer of either wines or distilled spirits. Mexico produces some very fine beers for which it might seek enhanced access to the Canadian market. The United States might well return to this issue in the context of a trilateral discussion, especially in light of the American industry's complaint under section 301 to force greater access for US beer to the Canadian market. As a result, Canada might have to be prepared to bite the bullet and deal with its quaint beer production and marketing practices even before trilateral discussions could be joined.[15] If not, this will be a politically difficult issue that may have to be resolved through some creative technical processes. Time, however, is on the side of a more rational system. The beer companies themselves are moving rapidly to diversify their production into other agri-food sectors and to rationalize beer production to the extent Canada's regulations allow.

Chapter Nine: Energy

The energy chapter is potentially the most difficult issue for Mexico for reasons that make it even more controversial than was the case in Canada. The Mexican Constitution (article 27) provides that the soil, sub-soil and resources of Mexico are a national patrimony and can only be exploited on behalf of the nation; they cannot be owned by foreign capital. Negotiating market disciplines for the energy sector, therefore, along the lines contemplated in chapter nine, could prove very difficult.

Mexico is a major producer of oil and, after Canada, the most important foreign supplier to the US market. The development of oil resources for export in the 1970s raised many expectations about the future of Mexico, and the fall in prices exacerbated many of Mexico's economic woes. Oil and oil-based products constituted some three-quarters of Mexico's exports in the early 1980s. The proportion is now down to about 30 percent, due to the combined effect of a rise in exports of manufactures, falling oil prices and mismanagement of Mexican oil exploration and exploitation. Canadian imports of Mexican crude never amounted to more than 3 percent of total Mexican exports and have steadily declined from a high of about 48,000 barrels per day in 1982 to a current level of about 10,000 barrels per day.[16] Mexico probably could not increase revenue from its energy sector today without significant outside capital and technical aid. Nevertheless, the energy sector remains critical for Mexico and makes the acceptance of market disciplines and export obligations politically difficult.

---

[15] Donald Creighton provides an amusing account of the historical development of these quaint practices in Ontario in "Wine, Spirits, and Provincial Politicians," in *The Passionate Observer: Selected Writings* (Toronto: McClelland and Stewart, 1980), pp. 65-70.

[16] Gabriel Székely, "Dilemmas of Export Diversification in a Developing Economy: Mexican Oil in the 1980s," *World Development*, vol. 17, no 11 (November, 1989), pp. 1777-1798.

Table 14
Mexican Exports of Oil to Canada and the United States

Sector	Canada	USA	Total	Canada	USA	Total
	thousands of barrels per day			value (billions of US$)		
1983	39.7	823.2	1534.8	-	7.5	16.2
1984	43.2	750.9	1525.6	0.5	6.7	16.5
1985	34.6	750.7	1438.2	0.4	7.0	14.8
1986	30.0	652.5	1289.8	0.1	3.3	5.9
1987	25.0	631.0	1345.4	0.1	3.5	8.4

Source: Adapted from Gabriel Székely, "Dilemmas of Export Diversification in a Developing Economy: Mexican Oil in the 1980s,"*World Development*, vol. 17, no 11 (November, 1989).

Despite similar interests as energy producers, Canada and Mexico do not compete directly in the United States market. Crude quality, distribution networks and other factors have resulted in regional oil and gas markets in North America.

To a much greater extent than in Canada, there is heavy Mexican government involvement in the energy sector. PEMEX, the state oil company, is a powerful organ of government policy and one of the most influential players in the Mexican economy. Unlike many other government-owned companies, PEMEX is not a candidate for privatization. The obligations in chapter nine, which in effect would require Mexico to move toward a much more market-oriented oil policy, would therefore involve major and controversial changes in Mexican policy. They would only become acceptable if they included the guarantee of major investment to make the sector more economically reliable.

In the course of Mexico's GATT accession, it signalled that energy was one of the sectors where it could not move as far and as fast as in other sectors and it has maintained that position. Even more clearly, President Salinas singled out the energy sector for special treatment during his June 9-11 visit to the United States, suggesting that oil might have to be excluded from the negotiations.[17]

The issue is largely one between the United States and Mexico, although the Canadian petrochemical sector also has a keen interest in nurturing a more market-oriented Mexican industry. Heavy investment in petrochemical production in Alberta predicated on free access to the US market would be undercut if Mexico gained equivalent access but continued to allow Mexican producers to gain ac-

---

17 *The New York Times*, June 11, 1990. He is also quoted as saying that "if you [the United States] are going to leave out maritime and telecommunications, we will certainly leave out oil, electricity" in Bruce Stokes, "Trade Talks with Mexico Face Hurdles," *The National Journal*, June 16, 1990.

cess to feedstock at below-market prices. Thus the Canadian interest may be less direct but nonetheless real. Fortunately, given the strongly held views of American interests in moving Mexico toward a more market-oriented approach, Canada can afford to let the US take the lead on this potentially explosive issue and save its leverage for issues where Canada is less likely to be able to count on US negotiating clout.

Chapter Ten: Automotive Products

At first blush, the automotive chapter would seem to be a difficult one. Further examination, however, suggests that the controversy is more likely to be symbolic than real. The Rubicon has been crossed and Mexican production is already being integrated into the North American auto economy.

The Big Three auto assemblers have invested heavily in Mexico in the past few years, sourcing parts and major components there, including engines, now the single most important item traded between Canada and Mexico. As a result, Canadian and US parts suppliers are under intense pressure to enter into joint ventures with Mexican parts producers or invest directly in Mexico in order to maintain their contracts with the Big Three. In effect, Big Three investment in Mexico has created a de facto trilateral trading block in the North American automotive sector: Canadian companies either source parts duty-free from Mexico under the terms of the Autopact or pay the GPT rate of 6 percent.[18] In addition, US and Japanese parts producers have invested heavily in Maquiladora plants – some 200 automotive-related Maquiladora plants are operating in northern Mexico – which limits duty liability into the United States to the value added in Mexico. Although the transfer of Canadian jobs to date has been minimal – Fleck, Bendix and Custom Trim have opened plants in Mexico – a free-trade environment between the US and Mexico would make Mexican investments more attractive for Canadian parts manufacturers.

Mexico introduced an Automotive Decree in 1989 to raise the Mexican auto parts industry to world-class standards. The Decree lowered import and investment barriers to attract capital-intensive, high-quality manufacturing operations to Mexico. Local content requirements are now down to 36 percent for assemblers and 30 percent for parts producers. Assemblers – GM, Ford, Chrysler, Nissan and Volkswagen – can now import vehicles to supplement domestic pro-

---

[18] See James P. Womack, "North American Integration in the Motor Vehicle Sector: Logic and Consequences," paper prepared for the International Forum: Mexico's Trade Options in the Changing International Economy, Universidad Tecnologica de Mexico, Mexico City, June 11-15, 1990 for a discussion of the probable evolution of automotive production in North America.

duction starting with up to 40 percent of export sales in 1991 and rising to nearly 60 percent by the 1994 model year.[19]

Given these developments, a more rational, integrated trade policy environment for the automotive sector would make sense and would not be all that difficult to negotiate. Nevertheless, the Canadian Auto Workers and their political supporters can be expected to use the excuse of trilateral negotiations to vent their frustration at the potential erosion of Canadian participation in North American automotive production, even though this erosion is being brought about largely by market forces.

Chapter Eleven: Safeguards

The safeguards chapter should not be a difficult chapter for Canada. Canada's principal concern was that it gain assurance that its products would not be sideswiped by US safeguard actions while retaining ability to take effective temporary action during the transitional period. Those objectives were met. Mexico will seek similar assurances from the United States. Given the structure of North American trade, Canada should not need enhanced safeguard procedures to guard against surges of imports from Mexico other than during the transition period, as provided in the FTA. The United States, on the other hand, may not be prepared to extend the same provisions to Mexico as it did to Canada. That will be an issue for the United States to work out, however, and will only involve Canadian interests peripherally. Nevertheless, should the US negotiate a different regime for Mexico, Canadian producers will insist that they be allowed to enjoy the same level of protection.

Chapter Twelve: Exceptions for Trade In Goods

Chapter twelve will have to be adjusted to meet specific Mexican concerns and may well lead to the addition of some Canadian and US exceptions that apply to Mexico. The specific issues that will need to be addressed, however, will not be clear until well into the negotiations after a much more detailed appreciation of the peculiarities of the Mexican trade regime. This chapter, in effect, provides the basis for dealing with difficult residual issues requiring either permanent or transitional exemption.

---

19 See US International Trade Commission, *Review of Trade and Investment Liberalization Measures by Mexico and Prospect for Future United States-Mexican Relations*, Publication 2275 of April, 1990.

Two issues that will require careful attention can be flagged now. Disputes between Canada and the United States under chapter 18 procedures suggest that the provisions dealing with the fishery and with the environment will need to be reviewed very carefully. Mexico has a significant interest in fishery trade and may not be as ready as the United States to grandfather certain Canadian provincial regulations. Similarly, the United States may want to review these exemptions. Additionally, heightened awareness of environmental issues has increased the opportunity for abusing environmental regulations for protectionist purposes. A tripartite negotiation may provide an opportunity to begin drafting international rules to curtail this temptation more stringently than article XX of the GATT.

Chapter Thirteen: Government Procurement

The extension of chapter thirteen to Mexico as it stands poses little difficulty for Canada, some difficulty for the United States and major difficulty for Mexico. The chapter builds on the GATT Government Procurement Code, to which the United States and Canada are signatories but to which Mexico is not. In its accession to GATT, Mexico made no commitments to open up its public sector to foreign competition.

Negotiations on government procurement would thus involve a three-step approach. First, Mexico would have to accede to the GATT Code or accept obligations equivalent to those of Canada and the United States. Second, Mexico would have to be prepared to undertake the slightly more onerous obligations of the FTA, particularly as regards transparency. Finally, the difficult negotiations foreseen in the FTA to expand government procurement obligations beyond what is achieved in the Uruguay Round will have to be taken up.

Considering the size and extent of the public sector in Mexico, opening it up to full competition would be a major step. While the combination of unilateral reforms and GATT accession has generally brought the Mexican import regime into greater conformity with those of Canada and the United States, Mexico has not yet taken similar steps to open up its public sector. Failure to take these steps, however, would not be a major obstacle to Mexican accession to the FTA. Canada and the United States themselves have not gone very far in opening up their public sectors. The GATT Code applies to less than five percent of federal government procurement in the two countries and chapter thirteen only increases that percentage marginally. The advantages of opening up procurement markets, therefore, remains a three-way challenge.

Negotiators in the Uruguay Round are seeking to increase the application and extent of the GATT Code. Canada and the United States are committed to continue negotiations on opening up procurement markets further in the light of the GATT results. The addition of Mexico to those discussions will make them significantly more difficult and will probably increase US intransigence. US politicians have over the years found government procurement preferences an important porkbarrel and are loathe to give them up without exacting a very steep price. US officials do not consider improved access to the Canadian market to be sufficient and are unlikely to regard the Mexican market as making up the difference.

Given this state of affairs, it would be in Canada's interest to convince Mexico to delay accession to chapter thirteen of the FTA until such time as it is prepared to accede to the GATT Code.

Chapter Fourteen: Services

It is possible that obligations similar to those in chapter fourteen may soon be developed on a multilateral basis in the Uruguay Round of GATT negotiations. The chapter, of course, provides a cautious set of obligations requiring that governments in their future regulation of specified service sectors will not discriminate between each other's providers of those services. Particularly if similar obligations are concluded under the Uruguay Round, Mexico should have no difficulty accepting these obligations nor should Canada or the US have difficulty extending these rights to Mexico. The Mexican service sector is not as developed as those of Canada and the United States and the comparative advantage clearly lies with US and Canadian service industries. Nevertheless, in the Uruguay Round, Mexico has advanced a generally positive approach in this negotiating group.

The question in trilateral negotiations, therefore, will be whether the anticipated extension of the obligations to existing regulations in specific sectors is of interest to Mexico. Mexico may well feel that it wants its service sector to grow somewhat before opening it any further to foreign competition. While the economic arguments for such a development are not very robust, the political case is strong and, as a result, this may well be an area where Mexico will seek temporary differential treatment. In the Uruguay Round, Mexico tabled proposals favouring the negotiation of a broad framework to govern trade in services but allowing for differential treatment on a sector-by-sector basis.

Thus the main challenge of this chapter for Canada is first to broaden coverage between Canada and the United States and second, to determine whether Mexico is prepared to go as far. Transportation services, for example, are not now covered. There is no contractual obligation on either government preventing

the establishment of rules discriminating in favour of local suppliers of transportation services. A further challenge will be to identify those areas where government regulations and programs in the services area currently do discriminate
in favour of local suppliers and to negotiate the reduction or elimination of such
barriers. This will be done on a sectoral basis and can also be done on a bilateral
basis within the framework established by the chapter in a manner similar to tariff negotiations under GATT. This is an area where it would be relatively easy to
provide temporary differential treatment.

Chapter Fifteen: Business Travel

This may prove the most politically controversial of all the chapters. Within a
Canada-US context, this chapter has provided one of the more welcome and
unanticipated benefits of the agreement. In the case of Mexico, however, given
the long history of illegal immigration, any relaxation of border crossing requirements, even when confined to business and professional travel, will elicit
strong opposition in the United States. At the same time, from a Mexican perspective, a better regime for business travel will be essential. As Canada discovered in the 1980s, the zealous enforcement of US immigration rules can severely
handicap legitimate cross-border trade and investment activity. Indeed, Mexico
may well regard the provisions defining business and professional travel unnec-
essarily restrictive and seek more relaxed criteria.

This issue will be largely one for the United States to work out with Mexico.
Given the distance between Canada and Mexico, the pressure of migrant and illegal labour from Mexico is a relatively minor issue for Canadians. Implementation of chapter fifteen required few substantive changes in Canadian law and
practice and its extension to Mexico, therefore, should elicit little controversy.
Additionally, Canada and Mexico have an existing arrangement on migrant
labour that could be used as a model for the movement of seasonal labour
between the United States and Mexico.

Chapter Sixteen: Investment

Over the past four years, Mexico has significantly relaxed its restrictions affecting
foreign direct investment and may be prepared to go further. Whole sectors of
the economy are now completely accessible to foreign investors while others are
open in partnership with Mexican interests.[20] Nevertheless, Mexico may want to

---

[20] See US International Trade Commission, *Review of Trade and Investment Liberalization Measures
by Mexico and Prospect for Future United States-Mexican Relations*, Publication 2275 of April,
1990.

guard jealously its <u>right</u> to regulate foreign direct investment and resist US demands that it not only translate its current laws and practices into treaty rights but extend these further. Again, this is an issue that is controversial largely between the United States and Mexico. Canada and Mexico will bring similar sensitivities about foreign investment to the bargaining table, with the major exception being that Canada in 1987 agreed to freeze its current regime on a contractual basis and roll back some restrictions.[21]

The difficult issues raised by this chapter may be somewhat ameliorated if there is a breakthrough in the Uruguay Round discussion of trade-related investment measures and Mexico joins any code to emerge from the GATT talks. Mexico has taken a fairly forward position on the TRIMs issue in GATT, presenting some innovative proposals and suggesting that it may have more room for maneuver than has been accepted by conventional wisdom. At this stage, however, it is too early to make any firm predictions about the outcome of the GATT negotiations.

Chapter Seventeen: Financial Services

Despite recent reforms, the Mexican banking sector remains heavily protected and Mexico may not accede readily to any requests to open it any further. Mexico recently announced gradual denationalization and relaxation of restrictions on foreign participation in its financial sector which, when in place, will permit foreign ownership in any one bank up to a maximum of 34 percent of non-voting shares, and in insurance, up to 49 percent foreign participation. The United States is likely to seek a more open regime but is not in a good negotiating position given the fragmented nature of its own banking system and the wide range of restrictive regulations at the state and federal levels.[22]

Canadian-owned banks, securities firms and insurance companies currently have no branches or subsidiaries in Mexico and have no plans to establish a presence in Mexico in the near future. Nevertheless, Canadian banks, while not necessarily interested in gaining greater access to the Mexican market for their own services, can be expected to support any negotiations for the same reason they

---

[21] An aide to President Salinas suggested during the June Washington visit that "Obviously from our point of view the key question is what types of services and investment should be included, while from the American side the labor factor is the most sensitive matter." *The New York Times,* June 11, 1990.

[22] See US International Trade Commission, *Review of Trade and Investment Liberalization Measures by Mexico and Prospect for Future United States-Mexican Relations,* Publication 2275 of April, 1990, pp. 5-10, 11.

supported the Canada-US negotiations: any agreement that expands business opportunities for their customers will expand business opportunities for them.

Canadian banks are heavily exposed to long-term Mexican debt, making most Canadian bankers wary of any new ventures there in the short term.[23] As Mexico's economy grows as a result of either a bilateral or trilateral free-trade arrangement, the likelihood of loan recoveries should improve (see table 17) and lead to a higher volume of trade financing (Mexico is EDC's fifth largest market in terms of total world exposure) and greater confidence. Canadian financial institutions might then take a livelier interest. As a result of this current low profile, however, Canada need not play an active role in extending this chapter to Mexico.

Table 15
Mexican Indebtedness to Canadian Banks
(millions C$, Jan 21, 1990)

Bank of Montreal	2,107
Bank of Nova Scotia	1,056
The Royal Bank of Canada	914
Canadian Imperial Bank of Commerce	375
National Bank of Canada	246
Toronto-Dominion Bank	215
Total	4,913

Source: Adapted from *Maclean's,* March 26, 1990, p. 43.

The provisions of chapter seventeen as written cannot readily be extended to Mexico. Canada and the United States accepted very specific obligations to reform certain laws and practices and committed themselves to future negotiations. Again, should the US insist that it wants to negotiate concessions from Mexico which, as in the case of Canada, the US will be largely unable to reciprocate, the issues will be largely between the US and Mexico and excite little interest in Canada.

For consideration, however, will be whether the United States is prepared, in the light of the changing international financial system, to entertain more extensive generic obligations and integrate this chapter more completely into the FTA. As it stands, the chapter has at best a tenuous connection to the rest of the agreement, both in style and substance. The institutional provisions of chapter eighteen, for example, do not apply to the financial services sector. Canada may

---

[23] The Royal Bank, for example, has cautioned Canadian business that it would only finance solid commercial projects. *The Financial Post,* March 19, 1990.

well wish to consider whether such an approach might usefully be pursued in the context of a trilateral negotiation, particularly if the results of the Uruguay Round are relatively meagre. Generic obligations would require a major revamping of US banking laws and open that sector to Canadian competition.

Chapter Eighteen: Institutional Provisions

The provisions of chapter eighteen as written are unlikely to generate any controversy should they be extended to Mexico, particularly in light of the reforms adopted in 1989 for the GATT dispute settlement provisions. The FTA provisions are very GATT-like and unexceptional.[24]

Nevertheless, the extension of the agreement to Mexico provides an opportunity to make the provisions of this chapter more robust and closer to the original proposals advanced by Canada. Experience in the first two years suggests that the United States may be prepared to overcome its traditional reluctance to enter into more rigorous institutional obligations. Canada and Mexico may well find that they have very similar interests and goals in strengthening this chapter. Additionally, there exists the possibility of significant advances in reforming the GATT institutional structure, a development that may help to reduce US opposition to stronger institutional provisions.[25]

Some changes will have to be contemplated. The addition of a third party to the agreement may require some adjustment to the procedures for the selection of panelists. For example, the agreement could be amended to require that the chairman of any panel comes from the country that is not a party to the dispute. More radically, the idea of a permanent tribunal might be considered. Both Canadian and US officials have been handicapped by the lack of independent support services for the agreement and the United States may now be prepared to consider the establishment of a modest permanent secretariat.

---

24 For a critical discussion of the Montreal reforms of the GATT dispute settlement procedures, see William J. Davey, "GATT Dispute Settlement: The Montreal Reforms," in Richard G. Dearden, Michael M. Hart and Debra P. Steger, eds., *Living with Free Trade; Canada, the Free Trade Agreement and the GATT* (Halifax and Ottawa: The Institute for Research on Public Policy and The Centre for Trade Policy and Law, 1990). A more general and reflective consideration of the state of dispute settlement in GATT and the FTA can be found in Robert E. Hudec, "The Judicialization of International Dispute Settlement" paper prepared for the fifth annual Ottawa Trade Law Conference, May 3, 1990 and to be published in Michael M. Hart and Debra P. Steger, eds., *Due Process and Transparency in International Trade Law*, forthcoming from the Centre for Trade Policy and Law.

25 The United States has reacted cautiously but favorably to Canadian proposals to work toward establishing a World Trade Organization (WTO) at the conclusion of the Uruguay Round should the results be sufficiently substantial.

Chapter Nineteen: Dispute Settlement for Countervailing and Antidumping Duty Cases

Mexico brings an attitude very similar to that of Canada to the growing US reliance on countervailing and antidumping duties to protect its industries. Like
Canada, it finds US laws and attitudes offensive and its procedures too easily
abused by US competitors. Between 1980 and 1986, the United States initiated 11
cases involving Canadian products; during the same period, it initiated 26 cases
involving Mexican products; nineteen of these cases resulted in restrictive action
of one kind or another.[26] Mexico's 1985 bilateral agreement with the United
States, making its cases eligible for the injury test, has made very little practical
difference. Very few Canadian cases have involved Mexican products. There
have been no countervailing duty cases and only three antidumping cases, involving a number of sources, that included Mexico.[27]

Partly as a counteroffensive, it has now equipped itself with countervailing
and antidumping duty laws. No Canadian products have so far been affected but
in the past three years, 15 Mexican cases have involved US products. As a result,
US traders have begun to worry about the potential impact of these laws. The
Mexican law, for example, allows preliminary duties to be applied within five
days of receipt of a complaint. Similarly, the determination of material injury appears to be rather easily influenced by political factors. The dubious quality of
the Mexican regime may prove to be a hidden negotiating asset.

The extension of the existing provisions of chapter nineteen to Mexico will be
viewed as a sine qua non by Mexico but is likely to excite suspicion and opposition in the United States. It is one thing to allow Canadians to participate in pan-
els that will determine whether US law has been properly applied; it is another to
extend that right to Mexicans who have little equivalent legal experience.
Antidumping and countervailing duties cases are not handled in a quasi-judicial
process; the concept of judicial review is not known for administrative issues;
and the principle of an independent judiciary is not well established. These temporary provisions were ultimately considered acceptable because they were
viewed as unique to the Canada-US FTA. Their extension to Mexico will bring
into question this important selling point and raise questions about how far the
US is prepared to see its trade remedy laws eroded by international obligations,
particularly with a country with a very different legal tradition.

---

[26] See Table 4.6 in Sidney Weintraub, *A Marriage of Convenience: Relations Between Mexico and the
United States* (New York: Oxford University Press, 1990), pp. 81-82.

[27] Inventory of cases as supplied by the Canadian International Trade Tribunal.

Even more controversial, in Mexico and the United States, will be the addition of Mexico to the Working Group charged with negotiating a subsidies code and a substitute regime for countervailing and antidumping duties. If American producers believe that Canadian goods are tainted as a result of a raft of subsidy and intervention programs, they will have even stronger views about Mexican products, where subsidization truly has been a way of life. At the same time, Mexico is unlikely to be able to take on the kinds of further reforms which would make the US more amenable to Mexican participation.

Nevertheless, the addition of Mexico to the Working Group might add strength to the Canadian position that while it may be desirable to place stricter disciplines on certain kinds of subsidy practices, this can only be achieved in the context of an agreement that places much tighter controls on the use of countervailing duties and eliminates the US penchant for unilateralism. Additionally, progress would need to be made to reduce the capacity of private interests to use antidumping procedures for protectionist and anticompetitive ends before Canada, and presumably Mexico, would be prepared to accept stricter subsidy disciplines. This will not be an easy issue, given the strength of US conviction on the need for private parties to be able to seek redress from foreign "unfair" trade practices.[28]

Chapter Twenty: Other Provisions

This chapter provides a grab bag of miscellaneous provisions, some of which address unique Canada-US issues and some of which are susceptible of broader application. In the first category fall articles 2005 (cultural industries), 2006 (retransmission rights), 2007 (print-in-Canada requirement), 2008 (plywood standards) and 2009 (softwood lumber). Articles 2001 (tax convention), 2002 (balance of payments), 2003 (national security), 2010 (monopolies) and 2011 (nullification and impairment) fall in the second. Article 2004, requiring cooperation on intellectual property discussions in the Uruguay Round, will have become a moot point but may provide a point of departure for a renewed effort by the United States to negotiate a substantive intellectual property chapter.

In the first category, Mexico is likely to seek an article equivalent to that of 2005 while the United States will wish to see an equivalent provision to article 2006. Mexico is unlikely to share the US view that the publishing, broadcasting

---

28 I have written elsewhere about the formidable challenge posed for Canada by the chapter 19 Working Group and the need for Canadians to take a more realistic approach to this issue. See "The Canada-United States Working Group on Subsidies: Problem, Opportunity or Solution?" paper prepared for a seminar on subsidies sponsored by the Ontario Centre for International Business, Toronto, November 1, 1989.

and similar industries are simply businesses like any others. At the same time, the United States has expressed concern about Mexican cable operators retransmitting Mexican and US local signals to areas for which the local transmitters have not paid royalties. Both issues proved controversial in the Canada-US negotiations but were eventually resolved; they will also need to be resolved in the US-Mexico context. Neither issue touches Canadian interests.

The extension of articles 2001, 2002 and 2003 to Mexico will be easy. On the other hand, Mexico may balk at accepting the obligations in articles 2010 and 2011. While these articles build on provisions in GATT (article 2010 reformulates article XVII on state trading and article 2011 borrows from GATT article XXIII), Mexico may believe that these articles address issues that are covered by its protocol of accession and its development status. Mexico continues to have a very large public sector and may not be able to go much further in its privatization drive. The obligations in these articles, therefore, could be onerous. Mexico's anxiety about these articles will in part be based on the assertion that it is not clear what the obligations in these articles entail. The only answer to this charge would be the development of much more concrete rights and obligations which take Mexican interests into account. Canadian interests could also be advanced in such a context.

The most controversial issue raised by this chapter, however, might well be US desire to include a substantive chapter on intellectual property. Such a chapter eluded the United States in the FTA negotiations. The United States could indicate that the price for Canadian participation in the negotiations would be such a chapter.

The difficult issue for Canada would be US demands regarding compulsory licensing and a North American patent system, i.e., an end to the national treatment regime that now applies and its replacement by the extension of US standards to Canada and Mexico. Mexico's position on such demands is difficult to determine. In current bilateral discussions, intellectual property protection issues have figured prominently and Mexico has been prepared to make concessions to American demands. Canada may, therefore, find itself isolated on this issue. On the other hand, the original quid pro quo, greater discipline on US section 337 procedures, may have been achieved as a result of the recent US-EC panel and developments in the Uruguay Round discussions on trade-related intellectual property protection.[29] Indeed, the results of the Uruguay Round may defuse this issue more generally and remove it from the regional agenda.

---

[29] A 1983 GATT panel, acting on a complaint from Canada, found US section 337 was not inconsistent with US GATT obligations. A 1989 panel, however, acting on an EC complaint, has

Chapter Twenty-One: Final Provisions

The final provisions of the agreement are unexceptional technical requirements and can be readily adapted to include Mexico.

Conclusions

Based on the foregoing analysis, it would appear that the most difficult technical issue involves rules of origin where vital Canadian interests are involved. Other areas that will require some ingenuity include some aspects of the chapter on border measures and the safeguards chapters. The more substantively difficult chapters include agriculture, energy, government procurement, business travel, investment, financial services and dispute settlement in the case of antidumping and countervailing duties. These are all much more difficult between Mexico and the United States than between Mexico and Canada. Three of these chapters – agriculture, government procurement and financial services – may lend themselves very well to differential treatment for Mexico without harming the integrity of the agreement. In addition, the automotive chapter will be symbolically difficult for Canada, and Canada may have to be prepared for further pressure from the United States on its regulatory regime for beer and compulsory licensing of pharmaceuticals. Canada and Mexico, by cooperating, may be able to achieve more progress on subsidies and countervailing and antidumping duties than either would be able to achieve alone.

The eventual success or failure of the negotiations, therefore, will depend largely on the degree of flexibility the United States and Mexico bring to the table on energy, business travel, investment, and antidumping and countervailing duties. These are also areas of priority importance for the United States and Mexico. The United States must be satisfied that the Mexican investment regime is both open and guaranteed by treaty and that the energy sector is more regulated by market forces while Mexico will only be able to sell an agreement domestically that provides it with more secure access to the US market and gives its nationals more open entry to the United States.

♦♦♦♦♦

ruled the opposite and the United States has agreed to bring these proceedings into conformity with its GATT obligations in the light of the results of the Uruguay Round on intellectual property right protection.

7

Thinking Strategically

International and domestic developments over the past few years have convinced Mexico's political, business and academic leaders that it is in Mexico's interest to negotiate a free-trade agreement with the United States. That interest has been welcomed at the level of the President and the Secretary of State in Washington and is not being discouraged by congressional leaders. As a result, Presidents Salinas and Bush announced in June agreement in principal to move toward negotiations "in a timely fashion." Now that Mexico and the United States have decided to proceed, should Canada join the negotiations? Would Canada be welcome at the table?

For Mexico, the positive factors in negotiating a North American accord are primarily economic: an agreement with the United States (and to some extent with Canada) would underwrite the transformation of the Mexican economy along the lines of the massive reforms initiated in 1985. These translate into some very specific objectives: elimination of US tariff and other barriers to the movement of Mexican goods and labour and a dispute settlement mechanism that will constrain US unilateralism, including the excesses of US process protectionism. The negatives are both economic and political: free trade would place additional strains on the weaker segments of the Mexican economy and raise stiff nationalist opposition. While economic reform is likely to stimulate political reform and strengthen democracy in Mexico, the nationalists do not share this perception. They will portray closer ties with the United States and the further privatization of the economy as solidifying the hold of the PRI administration and weakening prospects for political reform. The Mexican government will thus have very little room for manoeuvre. Canadian participation would help Mexico address some of the more difficult issues in the negotiations and would help to diffuse nationalist opposition at home.

For the United States, the benefits of a Mexico-US agreement are largely political: strengthening Mexican democracy by supporting economic reform, stemming illegal Mexican immigration, and facilitating cooperation in other areas, such as illegal drugs. These geopolitical factors are buttressed by trade and economic interests: the Administration wants to be seen to be resolving some specific trade and economic irritants, especially more open and secure conditions for US investment and intellectual property in Mexico, and gain commitments on energy pricing and supplies. The drawbacks are equally political: skepticism among some members of Congress and within the business community, and significant opposition from labour to opening the US market to low-cost Mexican goods in return for only modest and widely dispersed economic benefits. This means a tough negotiation about the details within a political context that is generally favourable and that will in the end ensure success. Canadian participation, while complicating the negotiating process, should help in managing some of Mexico's more extreme demands and at the same time further the long term prospect of hemispheric economic cooperation, as called for by President Bush.

For Canada, the immediate benefits of joining the negotiations are relatively opaque. Canada shares with the United States a desire to strengthen Mexican democracy and support economic reform and, more indirectly, to promote peace and stability in Central and South America. Similarly, Canadian participation would help to ensure that the agreement remains a building block towards an eventual hemispheric or even multilateral consensus on some of the most difficult issues on the global agenda. Such political and systemic factors, however, are insufficient reasons to proceed in the absence of clear commercial interests and benefits. The integration of Canadian industries into a dynamic North American industrial structure will help them to become more competitive and better able to penetrate world markets. Canadian-based industries would thus get the same benefits as their US competitors. It would improve the opportunities for Canadian producers to penetrate the markets of Latin America. It would also strengthen the government's hand in dealing with protectionist interests by further locking in the market orientation of the Canadian economy. Finally, it would allow Canada and Mexico to join forces in pursuing some of the objectives that eluded Canada in the 1985-87 Canada-US negotiations.

On the other hand, a North American accord will increase adjustment pressures on Canada's labour-intensive sectors, a point not lost on Canada's labour leaders who will be in the forefront of those opposing Canadian involvement. The most difficult issues for Canada – intellectual property and beer – involve the United States but need to be resolved in any event, either bilaterally or otherwise. In the debate to come, these short-term and more immediate issues will tend to crowd out the longer term benefits to the Canadian economy and make the issue difficult to manage politically.

The real issue for Canada, however, is whether it wants to participate, from the beginning, in the exciting prospect of building an integrated North American or even wider market or whether it wants to stand aloof from these developments. Depending on its scope, an agreement limited to the United States and Mexico could have profound economic and political implications for Canada. Failure to participate will make it impossible for Canada to help shape a tripartite arrangement that reflects Canadian interests. It would retard investment and restructuring in Canada to take advantage of global markets, reduce the ability of Canadian-based firms to penetrate the emerging markets of Central and South America and even erode some of the gains from the Canada-US agreement. Failure to participate could encourage the United States in developing a bilateralist trade policy with it as the hub in a rimless wheel of separate agreements, further undermining the open, multilateral trading system. Canada does not want to repeat the mistake the United Kingdom made in the 1950s and 1960s when it refused to join the integration movement on the continent. By joining almost a generation later, it found that it had not only missed some of the trade, investment and other economic opportunities of European integration, but it also had to accept an institutional structure that it had not helped to shape.

Given the consequences of failure to participate, it would appear prudent for Canada to seek to trilateralize the negotiations. The existing free-trade agreement between the United States and Canada would provide a convenient point of departure for such negotiations. It is a known text, couched in familiar language to meet commonly recognized objectives. While it would require some adjustments to meet Mexican aspirations, these are not so different from those of Canada and the United States as to overwhelm the basic thrust of the agreement. As was suggested in chapter six, these adjustments are manageable. Reaching a tripartite arrangement built upon the foundation of the FTA should also be attractive to the United States. It could greatly simplify potentially difficult negotiations and also make the results easier to implement. For Mexico, most elements of the FTA should prove a satisfactory basis for negotiation once it is accepted that Mexico's obligations could be phased in over a reasonable period of time.

There is a surprising degree of commonality of interest among the three countries, a commonality driven by both policy and commercial developments. During the decade of the 1980s, developments in all three countries resulted in a convergence of trade and investment policy, practice and interests that should greatly facilitate the negotiation of a tripartite arrangement. Canada and Mexico, as smaller economies already well integrated into the US economy, share many objectives. The United States and Canada similarly share some objectives as well as values, experiences and attitudes resulting from fifty years of trade negotiations and ever closer economic ties. Without these shared values and objectives, a trilateral negotiation would be very difficult.

Despite these shared values and interests, Canada has only a limited capacity to influence decisions by the two countries on the scope and timing of negotiations. Mexico and the United States are being driven by their own agenda, not that of Canada, although both governments have indicated they are well disposed to Canadian participation. Canada, therefore, needs to move quickly and decisively both to protect and to promote its interests. Said *The Ottawa Citizen*, echoing editorials in other leading newspapers: "It's no use wringing our hands. As Mexico and the United States prepare for the free trade talks agreed upon this week, Canada is sounding timid and worried. ... But Canada's wait-and-see attitude isn't doing anything to ensure it has an influential role when it counts – early in the game. Canada should push hard for a seat at the trade negotiating table now – and bring its own chair if necessary."[1]

Ministers are understandably nervous about yet another free-trade negotiation. The government is unpopular and rightly reasons that it does not need another controversial issue. Saddled with the failure of Meech Lake and the albatross of the GST, it would prefer a sure winner to another contentious issue. It appears, therefore, reluctant to move unless it is assured that there is strong support from business and the provinces. At the same time, Canadian ministers accept that if the United States proceeds with negotiations, there will be strong pressure on Canada from some US, Mexican and domestic sources to join. The government, however, remains unlikely to take a decisive step unless it is confident that the issue is not a loser.

A predictable opposition, both political and otherwise, has already put its cards on the table. In addition to the Pro-Canada Network's broadside against participation, NDP trade critic Dave Barrett has signalled the critical issue that will dominate the debate: "tens of thousands more Canadian jobs will be lost if

---

[1]   *The Ottawa Citizen,* June 13, 1990.

the government goes ahead with a free trade deal with Mexico."[2] Nevertheless, given the relatively nebulous opportunity and threat that Mexico represents, the issue will not gain the profile of the FTA debate. Discussion will be largely limited to the committed: the nationalists and professional worriers versus business and global realists.

The issue before Canadians, therefore, is whether to opt for the relatively low risk of participating in discussions from the start, thereby influencing their direction and content, or to opt for the higher risk course of watching from the sidelines, seeking inclusion at a later date if events warrant. Given the ambivalence of ministers toward a new set of free-trade negotiations, Canada's decision on whether or not to join the negotiations from the start will depend very much on the strength of signals given to ministers by Canadian business and the provinces.

The 1980s marked the first time that business on both sides of the border sent a clear message to the two governments that they were ready, willing and able to live with a bold new bilateral venture. Without that message, it would not have been possible to overcome the strong inertia of modern bureaucratic government or to alter the strong bias favouring multilateral negotiations. With that experience to guide them, business leaders should be insistent in making their views known regarding the extension of the agreement to Mexico. As long as those views are constructive and sympathetic to the significant problems that have to be overcome, they will be influential.

The 1980s also marked a quantum leap in the extent to which the provincial governments participated in the making of Canadian trade policy. Increasingly, issues within their jurisdiction or of immediate concern to them in the making of agricultural, industrial or other policies figured on the international negotiating agenda. As a result, they demanded and gained a place in the making of Canadian trade policy. Provincial governments were thus able to play a prominent role in convincing the federal government that it was in Canada's interest to negotiate a free-trade agreement with the United States. The challenge from Mexico offers them a similar opportunity to help set the agenda for the 1990s.

Fifty years ago, in the midst of depression, politicians and businessmen alike said enough was enough and started on the road to tariff sanity. Within ten years of passage of the landmark *Reciprocal Trade Agreements Act* of 1934, the United States had forged bilateral agreements with 27 countries, including two with Canada and one with Mexico. Ten years later, the US sponsored negotiation of

---

2   *The Toronto Star,* March 20, 1990.

the GATT. The 1987 Canada-US trade agreement, and the two acts implementing the agreement in Canada and the United States, provide a framework for starting on a similar road more attuned to the trading realities of the 1990s. The inclusion of Mexico in a tripartite free-trade arrangement can only be viewed as a positive and constructive next step.

♠♠♠♠♠

Selected Bibliography

Aho, C. Michael and Jonathan David Aronson, *Trade Talks: America Better Listen!* (New York: Council on Foreign Relations, 1986).

Aho, C. Michael and Marc Levinson, *After Reagan: Confronting the Changed World Economy* (New York: Council on Foreign Relations, 1988).

Aho, C. Michael, "More Bilateral Trade Agreements Would be a Blunder: What the New President Should Do," *Cornell International Law Journal,* vol. 22, no. 1 (Winter, 1989), pp. 25-38.

American Assembly, *Mexico and the United States* (Englewood Cliffs, New Jersey: Prentice-Hall, 1981).

Bilateral Commission on the Future of United States-Mexico Relations, *The Challenge of Interdependence: Mexico and the United States* (New York: University Press of America, 1989).

Bhagwati, Jagdish, *Protectionism* (Cambridge, Mass: MIT Press, 1988).

Brock, William E. and Robert D Hormats, eds., *The Global Economy: America's Role in the Decade Ahead* (New York: W. W. Norton, 1990).

Bucay, Nisso and Eduardo Perez Motta, "Mexico," chapter 6 in John Whalley, ed., *Dealing with the North: Developing Countries and the Global Trading System* (London: Centre for the Study of International Economic Relations, 1987).

Bucay, Nisso and Eduardo Perez Motta, "Trade Negotiation Strategy for Mexico," in John Whalley, ed., *The Small Among the Big* (London: Center for the Study of International Economic Relations, 1988).

Bueno, Gerardo, "A Mexican View," in William Diebold, Jr., ed., *Bilateralism, Multilateralism and Canada in U.S. Trade Policy* (New York: Council on Foreign Relations, 1988).

Callingaert, Michael, *The 1992 Challenge from Europe: Development of the European Community's Internal Market* (Washington: National Planning Association, 1988).

Cárdenas, Cuauhtémoc, "Misunderstanding Mexico," *Foreign Policy*, no. 78 (Spring, 1990), pp. 113-130.

Cline, William R., ed., *Trade Policy in the 1980s* (Washington: Institute for International Economics, 1983).

Curzon, Gerard, *Multilateral Commercial Diplomacy: The General Agreement on Tariffs and Trade and Its Impact on National Commercial Policies and Techniques* (London: Michael Joseph, 1965).

Dam, Kenneth W., *The GATT: Law and International Economic Organization* (Chicago: University of Chicago Press, 1970).

Dearden, Richard G., Michael M. Hart and Debra P. Steger, eds., *Living with Free Trade: Canada, the Free Trade Agreement and the GATT* (Halifax and Ottawa: The Institute for Research on Public Policy and The Centre for Trade Policy and Law, 1990).

Department of External Affairs, *A Review of Canadian Trade Policy* (Ottawa: Supply and Services, 1983).

Department of External Affairs, *Canadian Trade Negotiations: Introduction, Selected Documents, Further Reading* (Ottawa: Supply and Services, 1986).

Department of Finance, *The Canada-U.S. Free Trade Agreement: An Economic Assessment* (Ottawa: Department of Finance, 1988).

Destler, I. M., *American Trade Politics: System Under Stress* (Washington: Institute for International Economics, 1986).

Diebold, William Jr., ed., *Bilateralism, Multilateralism and Canada in US Trade Policy* (New York: Council on Foreign Relations, 1988).

Economic Council of Canada, *Venturing Forth: An Assessment of the Canada-U.S. Trade Agreement* (Ottawa: Supply and Services, 1988).

GATT, *Basic Instruments and Selected Documents*, vol. 26 (1979 report of the Working Party on Mexico) and vol. 33 (1986 report of the Working Party on Mexico).

GATT, *Trade Policy Review 1989: The United States of America* (Geneva: GATT, 1990).

GATT, *Trade Policy Review 1990: Canada* (Geneva: GATT, forthcoming).

Gilpin, Robert, *The Political Economy of International Relations* (Princeton: Princeton University Press, 1987).

Grey, Rodney de C., *Trade Policy in the 1980s: an Agenda for Canada-U.S. Trade Relations* (Montreal, C.D. Howe Institute, 1981).

Grey, Rodney de C., *United States Trade Policy Legislation: A Canadian View* (Montreal: The Institute for Research on Public Policy, 1982).

Hart, Michael M., *Some Thoughts on Canada-United States Sectroal Free Trade* (Montreal: Institute for Resarch on Public Policy, 1984).

Hart, Michael M., *Canadian Economic Development and the International Trading System* (Toronto: University of Torornto Press, 1985).

Hart, Michael M., "The Mercantilist's Lament: National Treatment and Modern Trade Negotiations," *Journal of World Trade Law*, vol. 21 (December, 1987).

Hart, Michael M., "GATT Article XXIV and the Canada-US Trade Negotiations," *Review of International Business Law*, vol. 1 (December, 1987).

Hart, Michael M. "Almost But Not Quite: the 1947-48 Bilateral Canada-US Negotiations," *American Review of Canadian Studies*, vol. XIX, Spring 1989, pp. 25-58.

Hart, Michael M., "The Future on the Table: The Continuing Negotiating Agenda under the Canada-United States Free-Trade Agreement," Richard Dearden, Michael Hart and Debra Steger, eds., *Living With Free Trade* (Ottawa and Halifax: Centre for Trade Policy and Law and Institute for Research on Public Policy, 1990).

Hudec, Robert, *Developing Countries in the GATT Legal System* (London: Trade Policy Research Centre, 1988).

Investment Canada, *The Business Implications of Globalization*, Working Paper number 1990-V, May, 1990.

Irish, Maureen and Emily F. Carasco, eds., *The Legal Framework for Canada-United States Trade* (Toronto: Carswell, 1987).

Jackson, John H., *World Trade and The Law of GATT* (Indianapolis: Bobbs-Merrill, 1969).

Johnson, Jon R. and Joel S. Schachter, *The Free Trade Agreement: A Comprehensive Guide* (Toronto: Canada Law Book, 1988).

Kock, Karin, *International Trade Policy and the GATT 1947-1967* (Stockholm: Almqvist and Wiksell, 1969).

Leutwiler, Fritz, et. al., *Trade Policies for a Better Future: Proposals for Action* (Geneva: GATT, 1985).

Lipsett, Seymour Martin, *Continental Divide: The Values and Institutions of the United States and Canada* (Toronto: C.D. Howe Institute, 1989).

Lipsey, Richard G. and Murray G. Smith, *Taking the Initiative: Canada's Trade Options in a Turbulent World* (Toronto: C.D. Howe Institute, 1987).

Lipsey, Richard G. and Murray G. Smith, *Global Imbalances and U.S. Policy Responses: A Canadian View* (Toronto: C.D. Howe Institute, 1987).

Lipsey, Richard G. and Robert C. York, *Evaluating the Free Trade Deal: A Guided Tour through the Canada-U.S. Agreement* (Toronto: C. D. Howe Institute, 1988).

Long, Olivier, et al., *Public Scrutiny of Protection: Domestic Policy Transparency and Trade Liberalization* (London: Trade Policy Research Centre, 1989).

McRae, Donald M. and Debra P. Steger, eds., *Understanding the Free Trade Agreement* (Halifax: Institute for Research on Public Policy, 1988).

Morici, Peter, "Regionalism in the International Trading System and Mexico-U.S. Relations," paper prepared for the International Forum: Mexico's Trade Options in the Changing International Economy, Universidad Tecnologica de Mexico, Mexico City, June 11-15, 1990.

Morici, Peter, ed., *Making Free Trade Work* (New York: Council on Foreign Relations, 1990).

Morici, Peter, *Life After Free Trade: U.S.-Canadian Commercial Relations in the 1990s* (Halifax: Institute for Research on Public Policy, forthcoming).

Nau, Henry, ed., *Domestic Trade Politics and the Uruguay Round* (New York: Columbia University Press).

Ostry, Sylvia, *Governments and Corporations in a Shrinking World* (New York: Council on Foreign Relations, 1990).

Pastor, Robert A. and Jorge G. Castañeda, *Limits to Friendship: The United States and Mexico* (New York: Alfred A. Knopf, 1988).

Petersmann, Ernst-Ulrich and Meinhard Hilf, eds., *The New GATT Round of Multilateral Trade Negotiations: Legal and Economic Problems* (Boston: Kluwer, 1989).

Purcell, Susan Kaufman, "Mexico-United States Relations," *Proceedings of the Academy of Political Science,* volume 34, no. 1 (New York, 1981).

Purcell, Susan Kaufman, *Mexico in Transition: Implications for U.S. Policy* (New York: Council on Foreign Relations, 1988).

Quinn, John and Philip Slayton, eds., *Non-Tariff Barriers After the Tokyo Round* (Montreal: Institute for Research on Public Policy, 1982)

Royal Commission on the Economic Union and Development Prospects for Canada, *Report* (Ottawa: Supply and Services, 1985).

Schott, Jeffrey J. and Murray G. Smith, eds, *The Canada-United States Free Trade Agreement: The Global Impact* (Ottawa and Washington: Institute for Research on Public Policy and Institute for International Economics, 1988).

Schott, Jeffrey J. , ed., *Free Trade Areas and U.S. Trade Policy* (Washington: Institute for International Economics, 1989).

Schott, Jeffrey, "A Strategy for Mexican Trade Policy in the 1990s," paper prepared for the International Forum: Mexico's Trade Options in the Changing International Economy, Universidad Tecnologica de Mexico, Mexico City, June 11-15, 1990.

Smith, Murray G. and Frank Stone, eds, *Assessing the Canada-U.S. Free Trade Agreement* (Halifax: The Institute for Research on Public Policy, 1987)

Smith, Murray G., "Canada, Mexico and the United States: Pursuing Common Multilateral Interests and Exploring North American Options," paper prepared for the International Forum: Mexico's Trade Options in the Changing International Economy, Universidad Tecnologica de Mexico, Mexico City, June 11-15, 1990.

Snape, R. H., *Issues in World Trade Policy: GATT at the Crossroads* (New York: St. Martin's Press, 1986).

Spich, Robert S., "Free Trade as Ideology, Fair Trade as Goal: Problems of an Ideological Approach to U.S. Trade Policy," *International Trade Journal* vol. 1, no. 2 (Winter, 1986), pp. 129-154.

Steger, Debra P., *A Concise Guide to the Canada-United States Free Trade Agreement* (Toronto: Carswell, 1988).

Stern, Robert M., Philip H. Trezise and John Whalley, eds., *Perspectives on a U.S.-Canadian Free Trade Agreement* (Washington: Brookings Institution, 1987).

Stoeckel, Andrew, David Pearce and Gary Banks, *Western Trade Blocs: Game, Set or Match for Asia-Pacific and the World Economy* (Canberra: Centre for International Economics, 1990).

Story, Dale, "Trade Politics and the Third World: A Case Study of the Mexican GATT Decision," *International Organization,* vol. 36, no. 4 (1982).

Stone, Frank, *Canada, the GATT and the International Trade System* (Montreal: Institute for Research on Public Policy, 1984).

Toro, Miguel Angel, "Mexico and Pacific Trade," in H. Edward English, ed., *Pacific Initiatives in Global Trade* (Halifax: Institute for Research on Public Policy, 1990).

Trigueros, Ignacio, "A Free Trade Agreement Between Mexico and the United States," in Jeffrey J. Schott, ed., *Free Trade Areas and U.S. Trade Policy* (Washington: Institute for International Economics, 1989).

United States International Trade Commission, *Review of Trade and Investment Liberalization Measures by Mexico and Prospects for Future United-States Mexican Relations* (Washington: USITC Publication 2275, April, 1990).

Vernon, Raymond, "International Trade Policy in the 1980s: Prospects and Problems," *International Studies Quarterly,* vol. 26, no. 4 (December 1982), pp. 483-510.

Vernon, Raymond and Debora L. Spar, *Beyond Globalism: Remaking American Foreign Economic Policy* (New York: The Free Press, 1989).

Weintraub, Sidney, *Free Trade Between Mexico and the United States?* (Washington: Brookings Institution, 1984).

Weintraub, Sidney, *Mexican Trade Policy and the North American Community* (Washington: Center for Strategic and International Studies, 1988).

Weintraub, Sidney, *A Marriage of Convenience: Relations Between Mexico and the United States* (New York: Oxford University Press, 1990).

Weintraub, Sidney, "The Impact of the Agreement [the Canada-US FTA] on Mexico" in Peter Morici, ed., *Making Free Trade Work* (New York: Council on Foreign Relations, 1990).

Weintraub, Sidney, "The North American Free Trade Debate," paper prepared for the International Forum: Mexico's Trade Options in the Changing International Economy, Universidad Tecnologica de Mexico, Mexico City, June 11-15, 1990.

Womack, James P., "North American Integration in the Motor Vehicle Sector: Logic and Consequences," paper prepared for the International Forum: Mexico's Trade Options in the Changing International Economy, Universidad Tecnologica de Mexico, Mexico City, June 11-15, 1990.

World Economic Forum, *The Competitiveness of the Mexican Economy: A Progress Report* (1990).

❤❤❤❤❤

Other Joint Centre-Institute Publications

Living with Free Trade   1990
Edited by Richard G. Dearden, Michael M. Hart and
Debra P. Steger

Due Process and Transparency in International   Forthcoming
Trade Law
Edited by Michael M. Hart and Debra P. Steger

Order Address

The Institute for Research on Public Policy
P.O. Box 3670 South
Halifax, Nova Scotia
B3J 3K6
1-800-565-659 (toll free)

Related Institute Publications

Understanding the Free Trade Agreement   1988
Edited by Donald M. McRae and Debra P. Steger

Canada, the Pacific and Global Trade   1989
Edited by Murray G. Smith

Pacific Initiatives in Global Trade   1990
Edited by H. Edward English

***Agricultural Trade: Domestic Pressures and
International Tensions***   1990
Edited by Grace Skogstad and Andrew Cooper

Order Address

The Institute for Research on Public Policy
P.O. Box 3670 South
Halifax, Nova Scotia
B3J 3K6
1-800-565-659 (toll free)